TRAINING NEEDS ANALYSIS TOOLKIT

A resource for identifying training needs,
selecting training strategies, and developing
training plans

Second Edition

Sharon Bartram and Brenda Gibson
SBG Associates

HRD Press   •   Amherst   •   Massachusetts

Published by: HRD Press, Inc.
                22 Amherst Road
                Amherst, MA 01002
                (800) 822-2801 (U.S. and Canada)
                (413) 253-3488
                (413) 253-3490 (Fax)
                http://www.hrdpress.com

In association with Gower Publishing, Ltd.

ISBN 0-87425-497-3

Typesetting by Michele Anctil
Cover design by Eileen Klockars
Editorial Services by Suzanne Bay

Contents

Preface to the second edition

For us, the process of writing is at once rewarding and challenging! Rewarding, because we learn again as we draw together our knowledge about a subject. Challenging, because we hope our style and practical approach will appeal to others.

We are thrilled at the success of the first edition of *Training Needs Analysis*. We know that the manual is used in different ways by professionals in the field; we have had comments from some about how Part One has been a real memory-jogger, and from others about how the instruments have given them a direction to follow.

The many helpful comments from practitioners and book reviewers have been incorporated into this second edition. We have extended Part One to give more guidance about starting and analyzing the initial information produced by the instruments, and included additional pro-forma outlines to assist you with this analysis. The section concludes with a summary in the form of an easy-reference flow chart of actions.

In Part Two, we discuss additional methods for collecting information, where appropriate, and have added a section on analyzing results to each instrument. Again, we have included pro-forma outlines to give you ideas.

We hope that this manual will continue to help you to put your training at the top of your organization's agenda and to identify realistic training solutions to improve the quality of the people you rely on to make your organization successful.

Sharon Bartram and Brenda Gibson

SBG Associates

Introduction

Whether you are an experienced or inexperienced training professional or the person responsible for 'people' issues, making your training count is the way to influence the future success of your organization. In order to do this, you must be able to match all training directly to the needs of the organization and the people in it.

This manual is intended to be a resource for analyzing training needs, selecting training strategies, and developing training plans to meet the identified needs. It contains reusable instruments and documents for gathering and processing information about training and development issues within your organization. This frees you from the time-consuming task of formulating methods for generating information, and allows you to make the contacts and build the relationships that are so important for winning support for training.

The manual is more than a set of instruments and ideas for documents. It has been designed:

- to provide guidance about the process of training needs analysis;
- to show you how to transform information into strategies and plans; and
- to explore a variety of ways to gather information at all levels of an organization.

In addition to helping you determine whether people are meeting known standards of performance, this manual will also be useful to you and your colleagues when you need to define and set standards that might not already exist or might not be clear to everyone.

Finding your way around the manual is easy. Part One examines the process of identifying and analyzing training needs. It starts by explaining why this is important and by showing the triggers to analysis that are your pointers to achievement. You will find guidelines for using the instruments (which appear in Part Two) to best effect, including how to brief your target groups so that you will succeed in gathering the information that will help advance your organization's goals.

Part One also reviews the different types of information the instruments will generate, suggests methods for analyzing this information, and lists the questions to ask to determine the appropriate training needs. A section on the benefits and potential problems of the main training strategies will help you to decide how the training needs can best be met. There are ideas for presenting training plans and a summary in the form of an easy-reference flowchart of actions. This section concludes with a series of documents to help you start, analyze information, and clearly present findings and proposals to others.

Part Two comprises the instruments, 22 in all. They cover:

- developing the organization
- organization climate
- managing resources
- job skills

Each section begins with an introduction that defines the area covered by the section, names and describes the instruments, and identifies the target groups. It also provides a checklist of the preparations you must make in order to achieve success. Each instrument conforms to a standard layout, making it easy to follow. You will always be given:

- the purpose of the instrument—what it is intended to do
- a description of the instrument—the format it takes
- the materials you require.

The instruments also set out methods for collecting information, with clear steps for administering the instrument by mail, conducting individual interviews or telephone surveys, leading group discussions, and so on. Each method is analyzed for its merits and potential for problems. This helps you to select the instrument most appropriate to your needs, as well as the best way of using it with your intended target group.

When you read through the sections, you will see that the instruments present a wide range of methods, including card sorts, questionnaires, profiles, and grids. This diversity has two important advantages: First, training needs analysis does not have to be repetitive and boring; second, if you find a method that works well in your organization (the card sort, for example), you can adapt some of the other instruments to this approach. Questionnaires can be adapted quickly by putting each question on a separate card so you can record the most appropriate way to generate the information you are looking for.

Gathering information is the first step and analyzing it is the second. Each instrument contains a section describing the appropriate method for analysis; most have documents included that will help you in this process.

Training and development requires investment in time and finance. Even with an analysis of training needs, plans can go awry. Sometimes this is because of issues outside your control and sometimes it is because the wrong solution has been adopted to deal with a training need. The best approach is to be prepared to monitor progress constantly and to make plans that are realistic and achievable. This manual will help you to carry out effective training needs analyses so that the investment your organization makes will achieve the desired results.

PART ONE

Analyzing Training Needs

Why Analyze Training Needs?

The analysis of training needs provides a focus and direction for the investment an organization makes in its people. Some training needs are obvious:

- Beginners with little or no experience in the job they have been recruited for will not be able to make a positive contribution until they have acquired the necessary knowledge and skills.
- Newly appointed first-line managers may have excellent job skills (that could be the reason for their promotion) but they will only obtain the best from the team after they have had the opportunity to develop their people-management skills.

Even when training needs appear to be obvious, it is still necessary to analyze specific knowledge and skill requirements in order to choose appropriate methods that will meet them. The new hire requires an individual plan showing the sequence of training, who the trainer will be, and how the training will be delivered. We know that the newly-appointed manager should have people-management skills, but what are the priorities? Is it leadership, team-building, or perhaps communications skills? Without the benefit of further analysis, it is easy to see how time and finances can be invested in the wrong areas. What are the consequences of this? Training costs money, but it does not add value to the organization because the people are not being developed in the best way.

Many training needs are not so obvious. Think about those people who have been doing their jobs for a long time and are competent at what they do. By analyzing their performance, you might identify aspects that can be improved or you might find potential that is not being used to its fullest.

When new systems or methods of working are introduced, is enough thought given to the impact they will have on people? Without analyzing the impact of the new systems and methods on the jobs people do, it will be difficult to help your workforce adapt to new knowledge and skill requirements.

Much attention is being paid to organizations that are going through a period of strategic planning during which they are developing business plans and forecasts to set targets for their future growth. How many organizations try to determine whether their workforce is capable of achieving the new and different demands this growth will lead to? By analyzing the current capabilities of employees, it is much easier to predict and overcome the potential barriers to achieving the company's new goals.

Because training and development is an investment, it is important to treat it as seriously as investment made, say, in machinery, new technology, or facilities. It is critical that companies first determine the benefits to be gained versus the costs and then decide on the investment. An effective training needs analysis will contribute to this by identifying training issues and priorities in a systematic way, rather than on an ad hoc basis. By examining individual as well as overall aspects of the organization, effective decisions can be made.

The benefits to you and your organization are:

- Investment in training and development will have a focus and direction.
- Priority training needs throughout the organization will become apparent.
- Appropriate methods for meeting these needs will be identified.
- Training will be systematic and planned but flexible enough to cope with ad hoc requests.
- The benefits of training will be measured against the initial costs.
- The contribution that training makes to organizational growth and success will be recognized.

There are consequences to not carrying out a detailed analysis of training needs. Whether you and your organization are going through boom times or slowdowns, can you afford to risk your investment in this way? The people who pay the price ultimately are the employees; without the right training and development, they can be your biggest liability. Trained effectively, however, they can become your biggest asset.

Starting your analysis

Before you begin your analysis, ask yourself:

- What is my role?
- What do other people expect of me?
- Does this organization know what a training needs analysis is all about?
- What type of training has this organization carried out in the past?
- What is the dominant style of managing people here?

What is my role?
Where do you place yourself on this continuum of trainer activity?

4

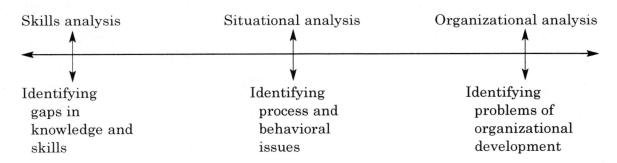

CONTINUUM OF TRAINER ACTIVITY

Skills analysis | Situational analysis | Organizational analysis

Identifying gaps in knowledge and skills | Identifying process and behavioral issues | Identifying problems of organizational development

If your role falls clearly into one of these areas, you can concentrate your efforts on examining information that enables you to operate effectively at your level. Perhaps your role is determined more by the problem; you move back and forth along the continuum as dictated by the needs of the problem. For example, one trainer who was asked to carry out an analysis of training needs amongst computer users initially operated at the skills-analysis end of the continuum to identify gaps in specific software knowledge and skills. The trainer discovered from the analysis that the computer system was time consuming for the users, leading to delays in response to customers and negative feedback from their managers. Improving software knowledge and skill would not solve these issues; they were situational and organizational. Knowing this, the trainer instead began to operate at these levels, gathering information that was more relevant to the issues.

What do other people expect of me?
How is your role perceived by others? Do they expect you to be the expert with all the answers? If your response is "yes," then this may have an impact on how readily others are willing to accept your ideas and solutions, and how much responsibility and ownership others are willing to take on for making your solutions work. If things don't go according to plan, and ownership is not shared, you may end up being the scapegoat.

Do others see you more as a facilitator? If your answer is "yes," then this can help you create an environment of collaboration; others will become involved throughout the training needs analysis process and share responsibility, ownership, and commitment. Perhaps you will have to work on influencing relationships so that you can create this environment of collaboration.

Does this organization know what training needs analysis is all about?
Look for evidence of how training needs have been identified in the past and consider the similarities and differences with what you are proposing to do with the instruments in this manual. You may need to inform people about training needs analysis so that they understand the process, recognize the benefits to them of targeting training more effectively, and accept the potential consequences of not following through with actions.

What type of training has this organization carried out in the past?

Whether you are new to the organization or are well established in your position, it is worth reviewing the information from personnel files and training records and discussing with employees what training has taken place. Take a critical look at whether training initiatives are linked to a business plan—this may affect the level of support in terms of finance and time that you can expect for training. See who has been involved in training and what type of training they have received. These considerations will help you to work out your strategy for implementing training needs analysis in a systematic way and suggest alternative solutions to identified needs. For example, if your organization thinks that training consists only of courses and you want to introduce the idea of workplace coaching, you will have to put time and effort into showing others the benefits of the different approach and the results that can be achieved.

What is the dominant style of managing people here?

The way people are managed usually determines how they respond to your methods of training needs analysis. If they are in an environment where they are told what to do, they may be reticent about giving their preferred answers to some of the instruments in this book; it is often safer to respond the way they perceive their "boss" will want them to.

People who are in an environment of genuine two-way communication where they are actively involved in decision-making are likely to be more positive in their response to training needs analysis. You need to identify the managing styles of your organization and the various individual departments and sections . This will help you identify the kind of barriers participants may need to overcome and work out who to influence to gain support.

Once you have a greater awareness and understanding of your role, your expectations of others, the training history of the organization, and your dominant management style, you can start on your training needs analysis. Ask yourself a few questions; some will be more relevant than others, depending on your role and the particular issues you are exploring. Helpful hints on actions you can take are given in the "Notes" column; use this space for your own thoughts and ideas.

Questions	Notes
• What is happening in your organization that might be a trigger for a training needs analysis? Potential triggers include: — taking on new people — internal promotions or transfers — new procedures and systems — new standards — new structures and relationships	

6

Questions	Notes
—new products —new customers —new equipment —employee reviews —requests from: your manager, senior managers, individuals —review of previous training plans —diversification into new markets —downsizing —commitment to training for specific employees, such as recent graduates —succession-planning activities —feedback from training events • Are there any negative indicators in your organization that might be additional triggers? Negative indicators include: —customer complaints —accident records —increasing numbers of grievance and/or disciplinary situations —high turnover of new recruits —loss of customers —increasing turnover of experienced employees —disputes —standards of work not being achieved —increase in waste/rejects/errors —higher rates of sickness and absence —decreases in productivity/ output —little interest in internal job vacancies • What external influences are there on your organization that might be triggers? External indicators include: —new legislation —changes to legislation —customer requirements	*Some of these triggers are connected. For example, could the increase in turnover of experienced employees be having an effect on loss of customers? Losing experienced employees and having to train so many new ones adds to the increasing pressure on managers. Is this affecting how they manage? Look at the increase in disciplinary matters and check evaluations for comments about this.*

Questions	Notes
—competitor activity —supplier activity —professional regulations/requirements	
• Who is likely to be affected by each of these triggers . . . —the people at the top? —senior managers? —departmental managers? —section managers, supervisors? —other groups (e.g., clerical, operational)?	*Create a matrix to show the links between the triggers and the people most likely to be affected. Table A (p. 27) provides a suggested layout for this.*
• Where can you find information about triggers? Try: —training records —personnel records —health and safety audits —sales figures —management information —appraisal documentation —customer satisfaction —trade journals —trade conferences and exhibitions —other trainers in similar organizations	*Make a list of all the potential sources of information under the categories of Documents, Records, and People to speed up the retrieval of the details.*
• How can you find information about these triggers? Try: —research reports, records, and statistics —examine the current situation, spend time in departments/sections to become familiar with the workflow and observe how people do their jobs —attend management meetings/briefings —arrange individual discussions with people at all levels.	*Compare the current situation with what was happening 6–12 months ago to identify changes.* *Record on a chart where work comes from, how it is processed, and where it goes. Table B (p. 29) provides a suggested format and a completed example.* *Avoid asking workers what kind of training they need! This is the quickest way to turn people off. Instead, find out how departments and sections work, and how they fit into the organization, the plans for the future, and the problems people encounter. This process is more likely to generate useful information.*

Use this information-gathering process as an important first step toward an effective training needs analysis. It will give you an impression of what is happening around you, but keep you from jumping to conclusions about what training is required. One company that telephoned customers to retrieve payments and arrears saw poor results and connected it to a likely need for telephone training. After investment in this training, leaders saw that the situation did not improve because the trigger had not changed. They then analyzed exactly what people were doing and found that the real training need was for debt-collecting skills. The investment paid off.

So far you have only considered indicators; their function has been to give direction to your analysis. If training is to have an impact on the organization, it is unlikely that you alone can investigate triggers, identify training needs, and find solutions. You will need to work with other people in order to:

- Define the objectives and scope of the training needs analysis. You may be the only person who has become aware of the triggers and the links between them that are worth investigating. There may be others who are aware of issues but find it difficult to pinpoint the changes they want.
- Identify and access the target population in the analysis. Not everyone views "training" as positive; it can be seen as a criticism of performance and, worse still, a punishment. The introduction of a needs analysis requires careful handling to overcome the skepticism and fear that may surround such an exercise.
- Agree to solutions about the issues raised in the analysis. The management must maintain good communication with newly trained/retrained people in order to incorporate the transfer of knowledge and skill into everyday working practice. The people who can influence the environment most are the trainees' immediate supervisors. Their commitment to the outcomes is vital to performance.

Focusing on these things allows you to plan what you have to find out, which instrument or combination of instruments will give you this information, and which people you want to use the instrument with. Consider using more than one instrument to generate information about the issue from as many different perspectives as possible. For example, a company desiring to improve its competitiveness can use the Focus on Perceptions instrument (see p. 77) in the section, "Developing the Organization." By combining this instrument with the one on Customer Satisfaction in the same section and the Work Fulfillment instrument from the section on "Organization Climate," they will create a comprehensive picture of their strengths and weaknesses, what their customers think about them, and how motivated their employees are. By identifying what needs to be done and the consequent training implications, the company is more likely to realize its ambition of improving competitiveness.

Decide whether you require a sponsor or champion to commit to the analysis; is there anyone who is pushing for action? A sponsor or champion should have sufficient authority to approve training expenditures and be capable of influencing others who have yet to give their full support. You must have their backing before embarking on a training needs analysis, as this type of activity always raises expectations. You will do more harm than good if you undertake an analysis, identify a training need, and implement a training plan without this support. The manager in one organization identified a need for training in decision-making skills. After organizing and running the first in a series of courses, he found himself being harangued by the chief executive for wasting time and money. In the chief executive's eyes, training in decision-making skills was not a priority, so it was brought to a halt. Such disasters take a long time to recover from and may damage the contribution training can make to an organization.

Additionally, the triggers will indicate whether your analysis will cover areas where standards are clearly defined (such as job skills and managing resources, Instruments 11–22), or where they do not exist or are not formulated (in the sections on developing the organization and organization climate, Instruments 1–10). These are not hard and fast categories, but do form a general rule.

Use the layout in Table C as a way of making notes about these issues for yourself. Keep a master of the layout and photocopy it each time you carry out an analysis.

Using the instruments
When you begin to use the instruments, it is critical to success that you: First, accurately identify the target group; second, decide on the method for administering the instrument; and third, brief the target group on the purpose of the instrument.

As a general rule, the target groups will follow the pattern in the matrix on p. 11.

Instrument	People at the top of the organization: — managing directors — general managers or equivalents	People who manage others: — senior managers of functions — departmental managers — section managers — supervisors or equivalents	People who do not manage others: — clerical — technical — manual or equivalents
1. Focus on perceptions	●		
2. Measures of success	●		
3. Organization profile	●		
4. Defining excellence	●		
5. Customer satisfaction	●		
6. Communications	●	●	●
7. Work fulfillment		●	●
8. What drives this organization?	●	●	●
9. Evidence of equality	●	●	●
10. Is this a learning organization?	●	●	●
11. Personal assessment		●	
12. Management match		●	
13. Managing time		●	
14. Managing people		●	
15. Managing expenditures		●	
16. How others see me	●	●	●
17. How do I see my managers?	●	●	
18. Analyzing jobs		●	●
19. Training needs survey		●	●
20. Task competencies		●	●
21. Working with others		●	●
22. Skills audit		●	●

Now that you have identified your target group, your next decision is how to use the instrument with them. Wherever possible, the suggested methods favor a face-to-face approach. This will encourage trust and openness in the process to make the information gathered worthwhile. However, this approach may not always be feasible (because of the numbers you intend to involve, or the time you and the target group have available, or the location of the target group). Alternative methods can maintain interest and momentum in training needs analysis. Weigh the options and choose the methods that best fit your requirements. You can make some adaptations to these suggested methods:

- Mail Survey—Adapt this to fit whatever internal mail system you use in your organization, such as e-mail and fax.
- Group Meetings—If you have a problem getting people together, particularly senior employees, videoconferencing might be a solution.
- One-to-One Meetings—If they are difficult to fit in, consider giving people time to look over the instrument and then telephone them to discuss their responses.

You can now prepare your group for the instrument. It is best to do this in a face-to-face briefing so that you can calm any fears individuals might have about the consequences of taking part in the analysis. Try to avoid what happened to the organization that invited a set of managers to a training course and used the course as an opportunity to carry out a training needs analysis. It seemed a good idea to send out a self-assessment document with the course instructions, but in reality most of the managers were alarmed that they would be disciplined or, worse, dismissed if they failed at any of the assessment tasks! What the company did revealed much more about the way people were managed in that organization. Be aware of what employees within your own organization are up against. By setting aside time for a face-to-face briefing on a one-to-one or group basis, you will help overcome these barriers. The areas you should cover during this briefing are shown below, with space for you to make notes about your ideas:

Briefing content	Notes
• Define training needs analysis for the group. • Ask about about the group's previous experience with training needs analysis. • Explain the background to this training needs analysis. • Clarify the group's involvement. • Stress why the analysis is important.	

Briefing content	Notes
• Explain the benefits. • Show the instrument. • Explain what it sets out to achieve. • Allow time for questions. • Explain how the information they supply will be used. • Stress the positive nature of *training needs analysis.* • Check for understanding of what is expected of participants. • Explain what will happen after the briefing. • Give each person a copy of the instrument, if appropriate to the method of administration.	

As you begin to use the instruments more regularly, you will find it helpful to monitor the success of the different methods. Whether it is a card sort or a questionnaire, the method may not be suitable for your group. Consider the type of organization you work for, what people are used to, the systems you have in place, and so on. Some organizations will be used to dealing with paperwork and generating reports; for them, responding to questionnaires will be acceptable (but not taking part in discussion groups). Others may prefer verbal communication to paperwork, and encourage creativity. Here, card sorts and brainstorming would be more effective than questionnaires and profiles. Think about the type of organization that you are in and keep a log of what produces the best responses. Work out how to prepare people for things that may be new to them and teach them how to adapt the instruments to meet your needs more closely. A suggested layout for your log is shown in Table D (p. 32).

Your familiarity with the instruments will also enable you to take advantage of ideas that spring from them. You might use some of the instruments as a basis for:

- one-to-one coaching
- discussion groups
- training course objectives, and
- training course content.

They are also learning opportunities in themselves. For example, anyone using Instrument 11 "Personal Assessment" in the section about managing resources will have already become aware of how they are using their time at work.

Open your mind to the possibilities created by using the instruments so that the effort you and your organization puts into them is worthwhile, thus generating quality information from which to develop successful strategies and plans.

Type of information gathered

Each section in the instruments serves a different purpose.

Section I. Developing the Organization: where the organization is now and where it sees itself in the future, and the necessary changes you will have to make. The information generated by the instruments will describe these changes and the appropriate actions you must take in order to achieve them.

Section II. Organization Climate: helps you to "take the temperature" of the organization and find out how people perceive what is happening around them, how they are treated, and so on. The information generated by these instruments will be a collection of these views and will form the basis for discussion with the people at the top of the organization.

Section III. Managing Resources: the styles and levels of competence the managers possess now, usually comparing these to best management practices. The information generated by these instruments will show how closely the managers' skills match the best practice and where there should be improvement.

Section IV. Job Skills: the whole range of knowledge, practical skills, and behavioral skills required by people to do their jobs. The instruments help to clarify what these skills are, who possesses them, and who needs to develop them. They also offer an opportunity to discover underutilized talent and skills. The information generated will show the spread of knowledge and skills throughout the company, highlighting areas for action.

Analyzing results

Having considered the purpose of using specific instruments to carry out your training needs analysis, you will also need to analyze the results. As a start, think about the following questions:

1. Do you intend to use the information . . .
   - . . . to show there is a training need?
   - . . . to refine specific issues when a broad training need has been identified?
   - . . . to develop a training course?
   - . . . to develop training plans?

2. Who is the audience for the information?
   - yourself only?
   - your training sponsor?
   - other managers?
   - the respondents to the instruments?

3. What level of analysis will they expect?
   - a detailed level, supported by graphs and figures?
   - a level where only trends are highlighted?

The information generated by the instruments lends itself to one of the following two types of analysis, or a combination of the two:

- Content analysis. (Create a matrix of the responses to the instruments given by the participants and identify the emerging themes for action. A template for a matrix is shown in Table E on p. 33.)
- Numerical analysis. (Do frequency counts, calculate averages, and make comparisons to identify trends and priority areas for action.)

The following matrix shows which instruments are most suitable to analysis types:

Instrument	Content analysis	Numerical analysis	Combination analysis
1. Focus on perceptions	●		
2. Measures of success		●	
3. Organization profile	●		
4. Defining excellence	●		
5. Customer satisfaction		●	
6. Communications	●		
7. Work fulfillment		●	
8. What drives this organization?		●	
9. Evidence of equality			●
10. Is this a learning organization?			●
11. Personal assessment		●	
12. Management match		●	
13. Managing time		●	
14. Managing people	●		
15. Managing expenditures		●	
16. How others see me		●	
17. How do I see my managers?		●	
18. Analyzing jobs		●	

15

Instrument	Content analysis	Numerical analysis	Combination analysis
19. Training needs survey			●
20. Task competencies		●	
21. Working with others		●	
22. Skills audit		●	

Each instrument contains a section on analyzing results, giving you tips and appropriate documents that will help you work with the information generated and summarize your findings. The suggestions may not be the only way of carrying out the analysis; their purpose is to provide ideas to start you off.

How to identify training needs

There will be some occasions when the information will require further consideration (see sections I and II). At other times you will be working with information that identifies an apparent training need. Sections III and IV fall into this category.

The instruments in sections I and II act as catalysts for finding out more information. If you wish to turn the proposed changes for developing the organization into training needs, use this checklist of questions and responses for each of the changes and actions.

Questions	Y	N	Responses
Does the change/action imply new systems, procedures, etc.?	✓		• If the changes alter how people do their jobs, some training will be necessary in order to use the new systems and procedures. Refer to Instruments 18–22 to find out what people already do before making a final decision.
Does the change/action imply new or revised job responsibilities?	✓		• If they fundamentally alter what people do, training may be necessary. Refer to Instruments 18–22 to find out more about job skills, and Instruments 11–17 to generate more information about capabilities before making a final decision.

16

Questions	Y	N	Responses
Does the change/action imply new or revised knowledge and skills?	✓		• Define the knowledge and skills required. Refer to Instruments 11–17 and 18–22 to compare the new expectations with what people do now before making a final decision.
Does the change/action imply a demand for more people?	✓		• Find out at what levels. Refer to Instruments 11–17 and 18–22 to find out the potential already available.
Does the change/action imply recruitment of new people to the organization?	✓		• Find out at what levels. Check that appropriate induction and departmental training is available.

Sometimes the answers to these questions will be "No," or the impact on people will be minimal. Not all changes and actions will generate training needs. There will be other ways of conveying what is happening (by organizational communication, for example). It might be worth looking at Instrument 6 (see p. 71) in section II to make sure that communication is effective. Using the instruments in section II to support other actions is especially helpful because they give a clear indication of what is happening to people.

When using the Section II "Organization Climate" instruments on their own, the checklist of questions and responses that follow will be helpful. This time, a negative response might still indicate a training need.

Questions	Y	N	Responses
Are the perceptions accurate?	✓		• Find out what the people at the top of the organization are prepared to do.
		✓	• Define the inaccuracy and investigate how it happened.

Questions	Y	N	Responses
Is this information telling us something that we did not know?	✓		• Define what has come to light. Describe how this affects the way the organization is run.
		✓	• Now that perceptions have been confirmed, find out what the people at the top are prepared to do about this.
Is it important that we change what we do?	✓		• Note the changes that will have the biggest impact on perceptions. Describe them in behavioral terms if appropriate (in other words, what people will have to do differently).
		✓	• With the help of the people at the top of the organization, work out why it is not important and prepare feedback about this.
Can we change what we do?	✓		• Find out who will have to make changes and in what way. Look at Instruments 11–17 to see what people do now before making a final decision.
		✓	• Investigate the barriers to change. Help those concerned to work out strategies for overcoming the barriers. Highlight the consequences of not changing.
Does this indicate that our employees will be willing to implement the changes we have already planned, to develop the organization?	✓	✓	• Proceed with action plans. Identify the barriers and ways of overcoming or minimizing them. Look at Instruments 18–22 for further information before deciding what to do.

It is important to re-administer some of the instruments in section II from time to time as a means of measuring progress made on achieving change and positively altering the climate of the organization.

Training strategies

Your next step is to work out how best to implement your training needs. You have several options to consider. The most widely used strategies are described for you here, together with their benefits and potential problems:

Option	Benefits	Potential problems
On-the-job training	• learning in the workplace • provides an example and standard to copy • useful for job skills training • low cost	• interruptions in the workplace • trainer capability • bad habits passed on
On-the-job coaching	• learning in the workplace • individuals solve their own problems • meets individual needs • useful for management skills development • low cost	• interruptions in the workplace • recognizing suitable opportunities • capabilities of the coach
Off-the-job courses	• groups exchange ideas • useful for job skills training and management development • safe environment in which to make mistakes	• disruption to workplace • unreal environment • can be costly

Option	Benefits	Potential problems
Projects	• learning in the workplace • combines with on-the-job coaching • opportunities for development clearly identified • low cost	• capabilities of the coach • fitting into existing teams • authority and responsibility must be clearly defined
Open learning	• learning at own pace • supports other methods • brings everyone to the same level of knowledge	• requires high level of self-motivation • can be costly

Your choice of training strategy may also reveal some additional training needs. For example, if you decide that on-the-job coaching is the best method, then make sure there is someone available with the necessary job and coaching skills. Remember, you will not always be the direct trainer. You will have to take these issues into account as you bring together all of the information generated: the training needs, as well as your selection of training strategies.

Training plans

At this stage you must first review your objectives and decide if you have achieved what you set out to do. Next, think about the expectations of the people involved—your sponsor, the participants, and other managers. Third, decide how best to present your findings and proposed training plans.

Here are three options:

Option 1   Write a report, circulate it, and ask for comments about the content.
Option 2   Make a presentation and support it with a report.
Option 3   Hold individual meetings to present the proposals.

Ask yourself these questions to help you make an appropriate choice. Use the space to record your own ideas.

Questions	Notes
• What did I say I would do at the start? • What is the communicative style here? 　—Do people usually read reports? 　—Are they used to attending presentations? 　—How much time do they have for individual meetings? 　—Will the same format suit everyone? • Who must be involved: 　—to give approval? 　—to give support? • Does everyone require the same amount of information? • How can I best monitor the proposed training plans?	

You will probably choose to produce a written document of some kind to illustrate your findings. Think about the various instruments that you can incorporate into your final presentation. Section I "Developing the Organization" includes action plans and analysis summaries for a report (see Instruments 2 and 5 for examples of these). Section II "Organization Climate" includes consolidated findings (see examples in Instruments 7 and 8). Section III "Managing Resources" contains action plans and consolidated findings that will be useful in your presentations. Instrument 12 combines both of these in one comprehensive document. Section IV "Job Skills" has forms within the instruments for use as the basis for training records and plans. For example, the task competencies chart in Instrument 20 provides the department's manager with training requirements, probably saving you the time and effort of producing any further documents.

It is important to make your communication clear and concise. This format might be useful for your reports:

Content

Summary

Introduction

Methodology

Analysis of data

Conclusions

Recommendations

Appendices

What follows are examples of layouts you might use to present your information (see Tables F, G, and H on pages 34, 35, and 36).

The first layout shows how one training manager has summarized training that has already taken place:

NAME	DEPARTMENT	TRAINING RECEIVED	TRAINING STRATEGY
J. Clay	Marketing	Responsibility at work	External off-the-job class
H. Wood	Stock control	Telephone sales	Internal off-the-job class
M. Tinney	Personnel	Job instruction Communication skills	External off-job classes

This can be used to review training throughout the organization, by department or by job.

The next layout shows how another trainer recorded training needs.

POSITION	TRAINING REQUIREMENT
Marketing manager Buyers Buyers' assistants Secretaries	Communications: 1. The importance of communications 2. Effective use of the telephone 3. Effective use of the fax machine
Buyers	Effective negotiation techniques
Buyers Buyers' assistants	Effective long-range planning

This layout helps the trainer identify training requirements that are common to more than one category of employee in the same department. It can be adapted to show areas of common training needs throughout an organization.

The final layout shows a straightforward way of presenting detailed training plans for departments and individuals.

Name/position	Training objective	Method	Cost	Time frame	Success indicators
• Inventory control manager • Inventory controller	To be able to use effective managerial and supervisory skills in the day-to-day running of the inventory control and supplies departments.	• Internal off-the-job course • On-the-job coaching	$150 0	Begin in next 3 months	1. Performance of team members 2. Relationship with team members 3. Quality of output from sections

Name/position	Training objective	Method	Cost	Time frame	Success indicators
K. Hughes	To use production planning and line balancing techniques in the day-to-day control of production output.	External off-the-job training course	$750	Before August	1. Daily production figures 2. Effective use of time 3. Standards improved by 10%

These comprehensive training plans based on training objectives clearly show what the training is intended to achieve, as well as indicators of success. Including the cost of this training makes it easier to decide whether the benefits to be gained justify the investment.

When you identify and present the training needs you have gathered from your analysis, be sure to present an accurate picture of what is happening in the organization. This will enable you and others to make decisions based on fact—decisions that will have an impact on all those who have been involved in using the instruments.

Summary

Follow the key actions described in Part One to complete a successful training needs analysis:

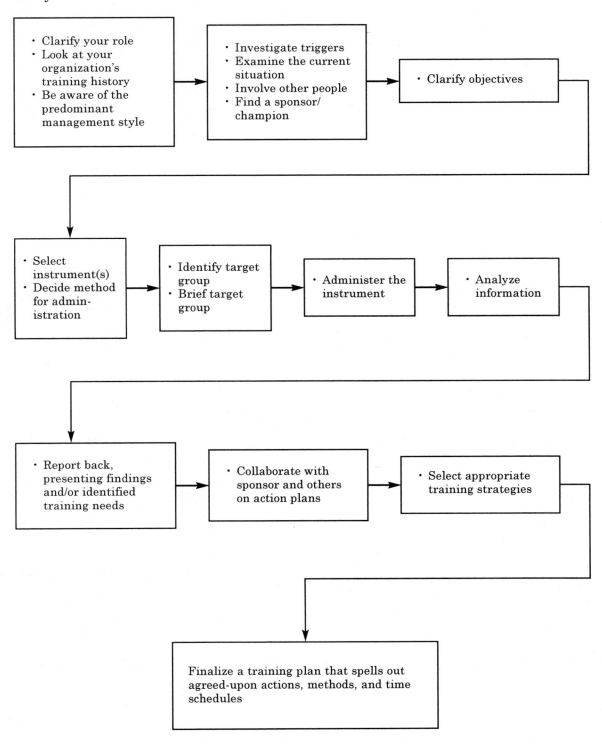

- Clarify your role
- Look at your organization's training history
- Be aware of the predominant management style

- Investigate triggers
- Examine the current situation
- Involve other people
- Find a sponsor/champion

- Clarify objectives

- Select instrument(s)
- Decide method for administration

- Identify target group
- Brief target group

- Administer the instrument

- Analyze information

- Report back, presenting findings and/or identified training needs

- Collaborate with sponsor and others on action plans

- Select appropriate training strategies

Finalize a training plan that spells out agreed-upon actions, methods, and time schedules

Table A: Matching triggers to people

	People at the top	Senior or function manager	Department manager	Section manager or supervisor	Others
Potential triggers —taking on new people —internal promotions/transfers —new procedures/systems —new standards —new structures/relationships —new products —new customers —new equipment —evaluations —requests from others —review of training plans —involvement in company initiatives —diversification to new markets —downsizing —training specific employees —succession planning —feedback from training					
Negative indicators —customer complaints —accident records —increasing grievance/discipline situations —high turnover of new recruits —loss of customers —increasing turnover of experienced employees —disputes —standards of work not achieved —increase in waste/rejects/errors					

	People at the top	Senior or function manager	Department manager	Section manager or supervisor	Others
— higher rates of sickness/absence — decreases in productivity and output — low response to internal job vacancies					
External influences — new legislation — changes to legislation — customer requirements — competitors — suppliers — regulations and requirements					

Table B: A picture of the current situation

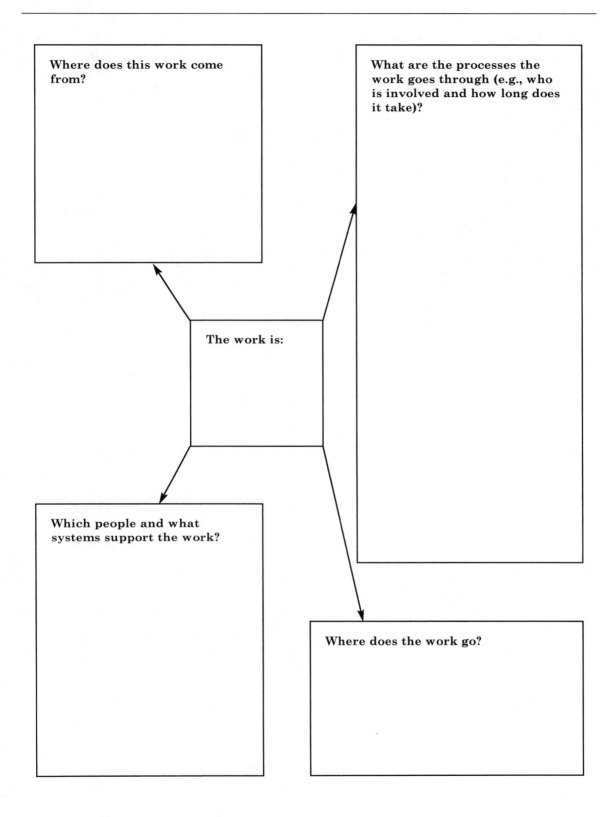

Where does this work come from?

What are the processes the work goes through (e.g., who is involved and how long does it take)?

The work is:

Which people and what systems support the work?

Where does the work go?

29

Table B: A picture of the current situation—example

Where does this work come from?

Direct from customers

The work is:

Booking vacation travel using a computer system

Which people and what systems support the work?

— Information technology department to maintain computer system
— Airlines to give flight schedules and seat availability
— Resort representatives to provide additional information about amenities and facilities for special needs
— Marketing department for brochures and briefings on new resorts and hotels
— Personnel and training to recruit new staff, maintain payroll, provide skills training

What are the processes the work goes through (e.g. who is involved, how long does it take, etc.)?

Answer . . .
Reservation clerks:
· Answer telephone calls from customers wishing to make vacation reservations.
· Check availability of flights and accommodations using computer system.
· If space is available, work out a price and tell customer the details and deposit requirements.
· Confirm the reservations using the computer system.
· Ask the customer to send in the deposit.
· If space is not available, sell alternatives to customer.
· Sell additional services (e.g., insurance, car rentals, excursions) to customers.
· Reconcile deposits received against bookings and confirm the booking on the computer.
· Send a computer-generated letter of confirmation to customer.
· Telephone calls with customers are to take not more than ten minutes.
· Each clerk must generate 20% of revenue through add-on selling.
· Supervisor must be informed when discrepancies with deposits occur.

Where does the work go to?

Via computer system to:
airlines; resorts; accounting; shipping

Table C: Starting your analysis

Who is my sponsor/champion?	Who are the likely target groups?	Which instruments will achieve this?	What do I want to find out?	What are the triggers? Are there links?

Table D: Instrument log

Instrument type	Target group	Number of people involved	Response rate	Quality of information generated

Table E: Content analysis—matrix template

Statements and questions						Summary of themes emerging most often
Name/group number						

33

Table F: Training record

Name	Department	Training received	Training strategy

Table G: Training needs

Position	Training requirement

Table H: Training plan

Name/position	Training objective	Method	Cost	Time frame	Success indicators

PART TWO

The Instruments

I

Developing the Organization

This section explores potential developments as seen by the people at the top. It contains five instruments:

1. Focus on Perceptions
2. Measures of Success
3. Organization Profile
4. Defining Excellence
5. Customer Satisfaction.

The target group is made up of the decision-makers in the organization. The instruments explained in this section will generate confidential information, and it is critical that those involved make careful plans to use it responsibly and effectively.

Focus on Perceptions reviews the organization's strengths and the areas needing improvement, and addresses the subjects of development opportunities, and potential hazards the organization must avoid.

Measures of Success sets organizational goals for future development and outlines the steps to take to achieve it.

Organization Profile shows how top managers assess the performance of the organization. A comparison of differing views will generate a wide range of material for discussion and action.

Defining Excellence specifies what the organization has to do to be the best in its marketplace or arena.

Customer Satisfaction asks customers to rate the organization's performance in meeting their needs. It will highlight areas of strength (to build on) and weaknesses that can lead to problems if not addressed.

Not all trainers are expected to be involved in organizational development, so first ask yourself: *Is this my job?* If your answer is "No," then move on to the next section. If your answer is "Yes," then be sure you have laid the groundwork for success in training needs analysis. Using this checklist as your guide, ask yourself:

Preparation	Y	N	Action
Have you . . . . . . identified and won the support of a sponsor from the top of the organization? . . . clarified your objectives? Do you know what you want to achieve with the instrument? . . . assessed the potential problems of using the instruments in this organization, and made contingencies for them? . . . selected the most appropriate method for collecting the information from the options given in the instrument? . . . prepared your briefing for the target group?			

Be sure you answer each question and elaborate in the "Action" column.

40

1

Focus on Perceptions

Purpose
To generate information about current organization performance and the potential impact of internal and external factors on future performance. To highlight the perceptions of different individuals about these issues.

Description
This instrument is based on a grid that uses statements as prompts to aid completion.

Materials
1. Sufficient copies of document 1.1.
2. A meeting room.
3. Table E (p. 33) for analysis.

Collecting information

Methods	Benefits	Potential problems
Grid completed individually.	— Easy to administer. — All points of view brought out.	— Large amount of information to be exchanged. — Harder to achieve consensus.
Group discussion.	— Consensus of opinion is easier to reach. Takes less time. Involves everyone immediately.	— Some points of view could be lost. — Dominant views take over.

Methods

Grid completed individually
1. Brief the target group on the purpose of the instrument.
2. Give a copy of the grid (document 1.1) to each person and agree on a time limit for completion.
3. Hold a meeting with the target group, allowing at least two hours.
4. Ask each person to present their completed grid.
5. Lead a group discussion to achieve a consensus about the perceptions highlighted by the grid, and create a plan for action.

Group discussion
1. Brief the target group on the purpose of the instrument.
2. Hold a meeting with the group, allowing at least two hours.
3. Together, brainstorm all issues and factors.
4. Prioritize these onto document 1.1, and ensure that each person receives a copy.
5. Create a plan for action that has the support of the whole group.

Analyzing results

Analysis type: CONTENT

Action
The analysis of the results is an integral part of the generation of information. However, you and your group may want some time for reflection before you agree on an action plan. A matrix to capture the emerging themes and patterns will help this process along. The template, Table E (p. 33), is suggested for this purpose.

Our organization is good at:	Our organization is hampered by:
Internal and external factors in the future that will provide opportunities for our organization to develop are:	Internal and external factors that could pose a threat to our organization in the future are:

Action plan
What must we do to tip the balance in our favor?

43

Reproduced from *Training Needs Analysis—Second Edition,*
Sharon Bartram and Brenda Gibson, HRD Press.

2
Measures of Success

Purpose
- To generate information about the future goals of the organization.
- To define how these goals will be achieved.

Description
This instrument uses a card sort approach to prioritize measures of success. The information then forms the basis of an action plan that lists the steps required to achieve success.

Materials
1. Sufficient copies of document 2.1, pasted onto cards measuring 3" × 2" and organized into packs.
2. Sufficient copies of document 2.2.
3. A meeting room.
4. Flip chart and pens.

Collecting information

Method	Benefits	Potential problems
Group work.	— Takes less time. — Builds on group commitment immediately.	— Gathering people together. — Points of view may be lost.

Method

Group work

1. Brief the target group on the purpose of the instrument.
2. Hold a meeting with the group, allowing at least two hours.
3. Organize subgroups to sort the cards (document 2.1) into priority order and to set achievable percentage goals.
4. Ask each subgroup to present its findings.
5. Lead a discussion to determine the priority measures of success and the steps to be put in place to achieve them.
6. Incorporate the steps into the action plan (document 2.2) and ensure that each person receives a copy.

Analyzing results

Analysis type: NUMERICAL

Action

Analyzing information is an integral part of the process of this instrument. However, if your group is unsure how to work with the information that is generated:

- Ask each person to state their highest priority and the percentage figure they have awarded.
- Compare this figure to their colleagues' evaluations, using a flip chart to record responses. For example:

NAME	TOP PRIORITY	%	RANGE OF PERCENTAGES

This analysis will help in two ways:

1. It will encourage discussion of the priority issues and how they impact on one another.
2. The range of percentages allows you to calculate averages; this will help members of the group come to agreement on a realistic figure that represents all their views.

We have reduced scrap by ___%.	We have provided all employees with ___ days' training.	We have increased our domestic market share by ___%.	We have improved product reliability by ___%.	We have reduced customer waiting time by ___%.
We have reduced outstanding debts from customers by ___%.	We have reduced labor turnover by ___%.	We have increased our client base by ___%.	We have increased investment in R&D by ___%.	We have reduced customer complaints by ___%.
We have improved our unit cost by ___%.	We have improved attendance by ___%.	We have sold our products to ___ new countries.	We have reduced product turnaround time by ___%.	We have improved product availability by ___%.
We have reduced distribution costs by ___%.	We have carried out performance reviews with all employees.	We have increased our product price by ___%.	We have extended our product range by ___%.	We respond to all customer inquiries within ___ hours.
We have improved our gross profit by ___%.	Employee suggestions have saved us ___.	We have expanded our business into ___ new market territories.	We have improved the reliability of delivery times of our suppliers by ___%.	We have increased the level of repeat business to ___%.

47

Time frame	Steps to be put in place	Measure of success

3
Organization Profile

Purpose
· To generate information about the current performance of the organization.
· To identify ways to improve efficiency and to achieve the goals of the organization.

Description
This instrument is based on responses to a series of open-ended statements about particular aspects of an organization.

Materials
1. Sufficient copies of document 3.1.
2. Meeting room.
3. Table E (p. 33) for analysis.

Collecting information

Methods	Benefits	Potential problems
Survey for self-completion.	— Takes less time. — Easy to administer.	— Ideas are not probed.
One-to-one interviews.	— Allows ideas to be probed.	— Time-consuming.
Group discussion.	— Ideas are shared. — Less time-consuming.	— Dominant views prevail. — Finding an opportunity to bring people together.

Methods

Survey for self-completion
1. Brief the target group on the purpose of the instrument.
2. Issue the survey (document 3.1) and agree on a time-limit for completion.
3. Collect the surveys and analyze by identifying similarities and differences in the responses.
4. Prepare a report that identifies the areas requiring action.
5. Arrange a meeting of the target group to present the findings and to gain agreement on an action plan.

One-to-one interviews
1. Brief the target group on the purpose of the instrument.
2. Arrange interviews with each person, allowing approximately one hour per interview.
3. Use the statements in document 3.1 as the basis for each discussion.
4. Probe the responses to clarify meaning.
5. Record the responses on document 3.1.
6. Prepare a report on the outcomes of the interviews, highlighting the areas for action.
7. Arrange a meeting of the target group to present the findings and gain agreement on an action plan.

Group discussion
1. Brief the target group on the purpose of the instrument.
2. Arrange a meeting to discuss the issues, allowing approximately two hours.
3. Use the statements (document 3.1) as a basis for the discussion and probe responses to clarify meaning.
4. Summarize the discussion by stating the areas for action that have emerged and gain agreement on an action plan.

Analyzing results

Analysis type: CONTENT

Action
Create a description of the organization and a matrix for each element of the survey: service, product, market, people, and control. This will make the search for themes easier and will help participants determine specific actions. Use the template, Table E, for this purpose.

Organization profile

This survey is designed to help you to think about your organization as it is at the present time.

Complete the following statements, giving as much detail as you can. Your information will provide the basis for deciding future actions.

Service

1. In describing our overall level of service, I would say:

2. Our customers would describe our service as:

3. When dealing with inquiries, customers would say we are:

4. In responding to customers' specific needs, our systems are:

5. Customers would say our reliability is:

51

Reproduced from *Training Needs Analysis—Second Edition*,
Sharon Bartram and Brenda Gibson, HRD Press.

Product

6. In describing the quality of our products, I would say:

7. In describing how our products fit the purpose they were designed for, I would say:

8. This organization's attitude towards research and development is:

9. In describing the appropriateness of the technologies used to produce our products, I would say:

10. In describing the systems we have of ensuring consistency of quality, I would say:

52

Market

11. The organization's position in the market is:

12. If I were asked who our customers are, I would say:

13. If I were asked who our competitors are, I would say:

14. Our customers choose our products because:

15. The untapped markets for our products are:

53

People

16. The organization's attitude towards its people is:

This is reflected by:

17. The qualities in people that we reward are:

18. In describing communication in this organization, I would say:

19. The standards this organization holds its people to are:

20. Employees' attitudes toward this organization are reflected by:

21. The main reasons for labor turnover in this organization are:

22. In describing the levels of absenteeism and sickness in this organization, I would say:

23. This organization identifies people with potential by:

24. If a person in a key position left tomorrow, unexpectedly, this organization would fill the gap by:

25. In describing this organization's methods of recruitment and selection, I would say:

Control

26. Financially this organization is:

27. When comparing our costs to budgets, I would say:

28. When describing the effectiveness of our way of monitoring costs, I would say:

29. The steps we take to improve cash flow are:

30. The aspects of the organization where we apply the most control are:

To sum up, in describing our organization, the main points I would make are:

4
Defining Excellence

Purpose
- To assess the performance of the organization against similar organizations and/or competitors.
- To generate information that defines excellence within the context of the organization and its potential.
- To identify how this excellence will be achieved.

Description
This instrument uses a grid to record the information generated.

Materials
1. Sufficient copies of document 4.1.
2. A meeting room.
3. Flip chart and pens.
4. Table E (p. 33) for analysis.

Collecting information

Method	Benefits	Potential problems
Group work.	— Shared ideas. — Shared commitment to action.	— Getting individuals together.

Method

Group work
1. Brief the target group on the purpose of the instrument and explain the importance of researching the activities of other organizations.
2. Carry out preliminary research on similar organizations and/or competitors; use libraries, site visits, and so on to gather information.
3. Produce a report on the findings and circulate this to the target group.
4. Hold a meeting to discuss the findings and to define standards of excellence for the organization. Allow at least two hours for this.
5. Give a copy of document 4.1 to each person and check for understanding.
6. Brainstorm to define the standards of excellence for each area on the grid.
7. Lead a discussion to identify the actions necessary to achieve the standards and ask each person to record these details on the grid.
8. Assist the group in coming to agreement on priority areas and deciding on the first actions.

Analyzing results

Analysis type: CONTENT

Action
The analysis of the results is an integral part of the instrument. However, if you and your group are unable to agree during the meeting, encourage each person to complete document 4.1; you will analyze them and report back the findings.

Prepare a matrix for each aspect of the instrument (service, product, market, people, and control) in order to highlight the emerging themes and allow for discussion to resolve differences. Use Table E for this purpose.

Standards of excellence	The facilities and equipment we require are:	The skills our employees require are:	The skills our managers require are:	The structures and systems we require are:
Service:				
Product:				
Market:				
People:				
Control:				

5
Customer Satisfaction

Purpose
- To generate information about customer needs and determine how satisfied they are that the organization meets these needs.
- To identify areas for action to more accurately meet the needs of customers.

Description
This instrument is a survey that combines two elements: the selection of aspects of the organization's product or service that are especially important, and then the rating of the organization's performance in these aspects.

Materials
1. Sufficient copies of document 5.1.
2. Document 5.2 for completion.
3. Document 5.3 for analysis summary.
4. A meeting room.
5. Flip chart, paper and pens.

Collecting information

Methods	Benefits	Potential problems
Postal survey.	— Increased sample size. — Ease of administration.	— Low return.
One-to-one interviews.	— Opportunity to probe information. — Guaranteed response level.	— Time needed. — Smaller sample size.

Methods	Benefits	Potential problems
Telephone survey.	— Allows for larger sample size. — Some respondents may find it easier to disclose details because they can be somewhat anonymous.	— Time-consuming if cannot keep to planned call times. — Lack of enough rapport to encourage frank response.
Group discussion.	— Builds relations with customers. — Customers can see your premises. — Opportunity to gather more evidence in support of responses.	— Might be difficult to arrange. — Other people will have to give up time (e.g., for tours of premises). — Restricted numbers may result in an unrepresentative sample.

Methods

Postal survey
1. Select a sample of customers and brief them on the purpose of the instrument.
2. Send each customer a copy of the survey (document 5.1) indicating the deadline for return.
3. Analyze the replies, using document 5.2 to record the findings.
4. Communicate the findings by written report to the target group.
5. Hold a meeting with the target group to discuss the findings and identify steps for action. Allow at least one hour.

One-to-one interviews
1. Select a sample of customers and brief them on the purpose of the instrument.
2. Arrange and carry out interviews with each customer, using document 5.1 as the basis for the discussion. Allow at least one hour per interview.
3. Analyze the information from each interview, using document 5.2 to summarize the findings.
4. Communicate the findings by written report to the target group.
5. Hold a meeting with the target group to discuss the findings and identify steps for action. Allow at least one hour.

Telephone survey

1. Select a sample of customers and brief them on the purpose of the instrument. Send each customer a copy of the instrument so that they can prepare for your follow-up call.
2. Agree on a convenient time to make your call, allowing about 20 minutes for each one.
3. Have ready a copy of document 5.1 for each customer.
4. Begin each call by explaining the steps:

    *   You will read out loud the list of items and ask the customer which ones they believe are important when dealing with your company.
    *   You will repeat their selected items and ask the customer to rate their satisfaction with your company's performance.

5. Check for clarity and start reading the items, placing a check (✓) against those selected by the customer.
6. Confirm their selections and ask them to rate their satisfaction with your company's performance in these categories. Again, place a check (✓) in the appropriate column on document 5.1.
7. Confirm the ratings they have given and thank them for their cooperation. Explain that you and the other managers will discuss the findings with the intention of improving service, and that you would like to review progress with them at another time.
8. Consolidate the responses from all the customers on document 5.2 for further analysis and feedback.
9. Communicate the findings by written report to the target group.
10. Hold a meeting with the target group to discuss the findings and identify steps for action. Allow at least one hour.

Group discussion

1. Select a sample of customers and brief them on the purpose of the instrument.
2. Arrange for the customers to visit your premises and provide them with suitable hospitality while you meet with them for about one hour.
3. With document 5.1 as your guide, explain the information you want to gather from them.
4. Write the items on flip chart paper. Encourage the group to identify which ones are important when dealing with your company, and place a check (✓) against each item selected. Note how many people make that choice.
5. Explain the ratings you want them to use to describe their satisfaction with your company's performance against the selected items.
6. Take the first selected item and record how many people are highly satisfied, satisfied, dissatisfied, or highly dissatisfied.
7. Before moving on to the next item, ask the group for personal experiences that support their ratings. Take notes.
8. Continue to record ratings and gather anecdotal evidence until all selected items have been discussed.

9. Thank the group for their cooperation. Explain that you and the other managers will discuss the findings with the intention of taking action to improve service, and that you would like to review progress with them. Consider giving your customers some small token to show your appreciation.

10. Provide a tour of your premises.

11. Consolidate the totals from the flip charts onto document 5.2 if you have more than one group discussion. Otherwise, use the information on the flip chart for further analysis and feedback.

12. Communicate the findings by written report to the target group.

13. Hold a meeting with the target group to discuss the findings and identify steps for action. Allow at least one hour.

Analyzing results

Analysis type: NUMERICAL

Action

Dissatisfaction of any degree on any issue requires action; your customers are telling you how you are meeting their expectations. To find the priorities in these areas, use the totals on document 5.2 and weight the values of the dissatisfied and highly dissatisfied totals like this:

- dissatisfied, multiply by 1
- highly dissatisfied, multiply by 2.

Rewrite the items in their order of priority according to their total weighted values, using document 5.3; the higher the value, the greater the priority.

Our organization values you as a customer. In order to meet your expectations of us, we would appreciate your cooperation in completing this survey. The information you provide will help us assess how best to provide a level of service that keeps you returning to us time after time. The information you supply will, of course, be treated in the strictest confidence.

The survey is divided into two parts: First, read the list of items and select (indicate with a check ✓) what is important to you when dealing with our company. Next, rate (indicate with a check ✓) your satisfaction with our performance in these categories. The categories are defined as: HS—highly satisfied; S—satisfied; D—dissatisfied; and HD—highly dissatisfied.

We look forward to reviewing your responses and plan to ask you to participate again as a way of checking our progress. We hope we can count on your continued assistance.

Thank you.

Item	Level of satisfaction			
	HS	S	D	HD
Quality				
Design				
Delivery speed				
Price				
Knowledgeable employees				
Post-purchase interaction				
Frequent communication				
Delivery reliability				
Performance				
Product range				
Receiving information about innovations				
Seeing the right people				
Locality				
Reliability				
Value for money				
Flexible customer-service policy				
Attitude of the sales staff				
Features and options				
Response time				
Things are right first time				
Other (please specify)				

65

Reproduced from *Training Needs Analysis—Second Edition,*
Sharon Bartram and Brenda Gibson, HRD Press.

Item	Times chosen	Total HS	Total S	Total D	Total HD
Quality					
Design					
Delivery speed					
Price					
Knowledgeable employees					
Post-purchase interaction					
Frequent communication					
Delivery reliability					
Performance					
Product range					
Receiving information about innovations					
Seeing the right people					
Locality					
Reliability					
Value for money					
Flexible customer-service policy					
Attitude of the sales staff					
Features and options					
Response time					
Things are right first time					
Other (please specify)					

Customer satisfaction—priorities for action

Document 5.3

Item	Times chosen	Weighted value	Priority

II
Organization Climate

This section measures employee perceptions of the organization. Senior leaders within the organization who are committed to positive change will address the issues identified by the instruments; the way an organization is perceived by its employees is, after all, an important indicator of how people outside might also see it, and is a factor in its long-term success. There are five instruments:

6. Communications
7. Work Fulfillment
8. What Drives This Organization?
9. Evidence of Equality
10. Is This a Learning Organization?

The organization's entire workforce make up the target group, but the initiative for this work must come from the top. It would be reckless to use these instruments without that support because the questions will raise people's consciousness about what is going on around them and raise expectations that things will change. Failure to institute positive changes will adversely impact the organization and take a long time to recover from.

Communications reflects the views of employees about any improvements the organization may make.

Work Fulfillment highlights the levels of job satisfaction within the organization, as well as attitudes towards authority, work planning, communications, and work methods.

What Drives This Organization? shows whether the managers at the top are consistently conveying the values of the organization to the workforce.

Evidence of Equality researches the organization's achievements in providing equality of opportunity in all aspects. It shows where equal treatment exists and where there have been instances of direct or indirect discrimination.

Is This a Learning Organization? examines employees' perceptions of how the organization treats them and their futures.

Not all trainers are expected to be involved in creating an organizational climate; ask yourself if it is part of your job. If it isn't, move on to the next section. If it is, be sure you have made the preparations necessary to the success of this aspect of training needs analysis. Using this checklist as your guide. Have you . . .

Preparation	Y	N	Action
. . . identified and won the support of the appropriate sponsor?			
. . . clarified your objectives? Do you know what you want to achieve by using the instrument?			
. . . assessed the potential problems of using the instruments in this organization, and made contingencies for them?			
. . . assessed the potential problems of using the instruments with this target group, and made contingencies for them?			
. . . considered the expectations that participation will raise, and discussed them with your sponsor and other managers?			
. . . selected the best method of collecting the information from the options given in the instrument?			
. . . prepared your briefing for the target group?			

6

Communications

Purpose
- To generate information about how communication in the organization is perceived.
- To collect ideas from employees on how communication might be improved.
- To identify areas of the organization that will help or hinder the achievement of these objectives.

Description
This instrument uses brainstorming techniques to provide a quantity of ideas, which are then put into priority order and analyzed.

Materials
1. Sufficient copies of document 6.1.
2. Prepared flip charts (document 6.2).
3. Copy of document 6.3 for reference.
4. Meeting room.
5. Flip chart paper, pens, and adhesive-backed stars or other shapes (available from office supply stores).
6. Table E (p. 33) for analysis.

Collecting information

Methods	Benefits	Potential problems
Group discussions: — all employees at each level; — sampling of employees at each level;	— Generates solutions. — Highly participative. — A safe way to express opinions.	— Time needed to assemble groups and complete the activity. — Solutions could be contrary to current management styles.

continued

71

Methods	Benefits	Potential problems
— mixture of levels across a function or department.		
Group discussions to establish priorities, followed by a meeting with management to identify changes.	— Easy to administer. — Involves decision-makers earlier in the process.	— Employees not involved in identifying changes, so could limit commitment.

Methods

Group discussion for whole process
1. Brief the target group on the purpose of the instrument.
2. Arrange meetings with groups of between 10 and 15 people, allowing one hour per meeting.
3. During each meeting, distribute document 6.1 and explain the brainstorming technique. You might find a warm-up topic useful, such as "Uses for a ball of string." This ensures understanding of the technique and helps to remove inhibitions.
4. Using your prepared flip chart A (see document 6.2) begin the brainstorm, maintaining the momentum until the group runs out of ideas.
5. Evaluate the brainstorm list by removing duplicated ideas and asking the group for links between ideas. Write the consolidated list onto a new flip chart.
6. Give each group member 10 adhesive stars; these are to be placed next to the ten most important ideas for improvements. More than one star can be given to an idea. If someone believes one improvement is more important than any other, they can allocate all ten stars to it.
7. Add up the total number of stars for each improvement idea and under-line the top five with the highest scores. Ask the group to record them on document 6.1.
8. Using your prepared flip charts B, C, and D (see document 6.2), ask for con-tributions relating to each heading. The questions on document 6.3 are suggested prompts for this discussion.
9. Close the meeting by explaining that the information generated by each group will be consolidated into a report about which they will receive feedback.
10. Produce a report showing the trends in suggested improvements and the improvements that are seen as priorities. Include a summary, changes to be made, benefits to be realized, and potential problems to be overcome to achieve the improvements.

11. Distribute and discuss the findings with senior managers and decision-makers, and come to an agreement on action.
12. Give feedback to the target group.

Group discussions to establish priorities, followed by a meeting with management to identify changes
Follow steps 1 to 7 and conclude the group meetings at this point.
Then:
8. Arrange meetings with managers to assess the priority improvements suggested by the groups. Use your prepared flip charts B, C, and D (see document 6.2) as a framework for discussion.
9. Agree on action to put the improvements in place.
10. Produce a report that summarizes the outcomes, and provide feedback to the target groups.

Analyzing results

Analysis type: CONTENT

Action
You have already used some numerical analysis as part of the instrument. The information for your content analysis is recorded on flip charts B, C, and D. Find the main themes emerging from the discussions and create a matrix to summarize the range of responses given. Use Table E for this purpose.

Brainstorming

Brainstorming is a technique used to generate a number of ideas about a particular topic. Contribute your ideas freely, whatever they are, because the more ideas that are generated, the more likely you are to find quality solutions to the issues.

Rules of brainstorming:

- Do not be critical of any idea.
- Defer any judgments about ideas.
- Quantity (of ideas) is all-important.
- Building on ideas is useful.
- Allow freewheeling thought and wild ideas.

Record the priority ideas from your group's brainstorming exercise on this topic:

"Improving communications here"

Top priority: _____

_____

_____

_____

_____

Prepare your flip charts to look like these:

A

> Ways of improving
> communications here

B

> What changes would you
> make to achieve the priority
> improvements?

C

> What benefits are to be
> gained from the priority
> improvements?

D

> What potential problems
> must be overcome in order to
> achieve the priority
> improvements?

Question prompts

- How is news and information from the top of the organization usually disseminated?
- How do we use indirect methods of communication, such as bulletin boards and newsletters, to spread news and information?
- What opportunities are there to express your opinion?
- How effective are we at communicating the message to the right people at the right time?
- Is there a "grapevine" working here?
- What feedback do you receive if, for instance, you make a formal suggestion for improvement?
- How are you encouraged to pass along your suggestions to management?
- Is communication on a "need to know" basis only?
- How regularly do we communicate here?
- What types of communication do we use here?

  Giving orders?
  Providing feedback on results and future plans?
  Soliciting your views?
  Involving you in decisions?

7
Work Fulfillment

Purpose
To generate information about job satisfaction and employee attitudes regarding how authority, work-planning, communications, and work methods operate at departmental and organizational levels.

Description
This instrument is a survey requiring employees to consider twenty paired statements in relation to their individual work situations. By comparing and then rating the statements, each employee can describe their situation as they see it.

Materials
1. Sufficient copies of documents 7.1a and 7.1b.
2. Document 7.2.
3. A meeting room.

Collecting information

Methods	Benefits	Potential problems
Postal survey.	— Easy to administer. — Generates information quickly.	— Poor response rate. — Worries about confidentiality.
Survey completed individually, followed by individual meetings.	— Able to confirm understanding. — Reassure about confidentiality.	— Time-consuming.

Methods	Benefits	Potential problems
Survey completed individually, followed by group meetings.	— Able to confirm understanding. — Reassure about confidentiality. — Explore common ground.	— Disruptive to workplace. — Minority views overlooked.
Survey used as basis for individual discussion.	— Encourages disclosure.	— Time-consuming
Survey used as basis for group discussion.	— Speeds up gathering of information	— Stifles disclosure. — Dominant views suppress others.

Methods

Postal survey
1. Decide whether to collect information on a departmental basis (document 7.1a) or an organizational basis (document 7.1b).
2. Brief the target group on the purpose of the instrument, stressing that there will be feedback on the findings and agreed-upon actions.
3. Distribute a copy of the appropriate survey (document 7.1a or 7.1b) to each person and agree on a time schedule for completion and return.
4. Analyze the completed surveys using document 7.2. Present the findings to senior managers for discussion and decision.

Survey completed individually, followed by individual meetings
Follow steps 1 and 2 above.
Then:
3. Distribute a copy of the appropriate survey (document 7.1a or 7.1b) to each person and arrange for a follow-up meeting. Allow up to 45 minutes per meeting.
4. During the meeting, review the person's completed survey and ask them to explain the reasons for their ratings and suggest improvements. Record any comments.
5. Make a copy of each completed survey before closing the meeting.
6. When all meetings are complete, analyze the surveys and additional comments using document 7.2.

Survey completed individually, followed by group meetings
Follow the six steps described above, organizing group meetings of not more than 12 people and allowing up to 90 minutes per meeting.

Survey used as basis for individual discussion
Follow steps 1 and 2 above.
Then:
  3. Arrange a meeting with each person, allowing one hour per meeting.
  4. During the meetings, present the survey (either document 7.1a or 7.1b) to each person and ask them to respond, explaining the reasons for their ratings and suggesting improvements. Record any comments.

Follow steps 5 and 6 above.

Survey used as basis for group discussion
Follow steps 1 and 2 above.
Then:
  3. Arrange a series of group meetings with not more than 12 people and allow up to 90 minutes per meeting.
  4. During the meetings, distribute the survey (document 7.1a or 7.1b) to each person. Ask them to respond and explore the reasons behind their ratings and suggestions for improvements. Record any comments.
  5. When all the meetings have taken place, analyze the range of responses to the survey and additional comments, using document 7.2. Present your findings to senior managers for discussion and decision.

Analyzing results

Analysis type: NUMERICAL

Action
The instructions for using this instrument provide the basis for your analysis. You will carry out frequency counts to determine the number of people rating a pair of statements in a particular way (document 7.2). For more impact, create a chart of the findings for each paired statement to show the differences and similarities in the responses. For example, if there are 20 people in the survey and seven of them rated statement 1 as 1, five of them as 2, two of them as 4, three of them as 5, and three of them as 6, record this on document 7.2 as follows:

Paired statement number	Number of people choosing a rating of:					
	1	2	3	4	5	6
Job satisfaction 1	▤	▤		▤	▤	▤

You could also compare the ratings between responses to the organizational survey and the departmental survey to see if there are underlying trends.

Thinking about your department, read the following paired statements and put a check (✓) at the point on the scale corresponding most closely to the situation as you see it.

        1   2   3   4   5   6

1. I am given feedback about my job performance and advice on how to improve it. | | I am not given the opportunity to voice difficulties about my job and I am not informed sufficiently about my performance.

2. Decision-making is carried out by consultation with the entire department. | | Decision-making involves only the few people in authority within the department.

3. My job is clearly defined and I understand what I am expected to do. | | My job overlaps with others, and I am not clear about what I have to do.

4. Work is planned so that time schedules can be met. | | Work planning is haphazard, and sometimes deadlines don't get met.

5. Objectives are clearly defined for my department. | | I do not have a clear idea of my department's goals and objectives.

6. I have a clear understanding of the goals of the other work groups within the department. | | No one here knows exactly what other people are doing.

7. There is a well-defined chain of command here. I know who to take my problems to. | | The chain of command is not well-defined; I am not clear who to take my problems to.

8. I feel I am encouraged to develop my potential and that I am making progress. | | I feel I am not encouraged to develop my potential, and consequently I am not making progress.

81

	1	2	3	4	5	6	

9. The different sections within the department work well together, achieving a high standard of effectiveness.

There is considerable friction and lack of cooperation between different sections in the department and we are not achieving a high standard of effectiveness.

10. I am able to use my own initiative to achieve results when tackling the duties of my job.

I work within the constraints of predetermined procedures to achieve results.

11. OPEN communications: motives, objectives, and plans are discussed openly.

CLOSED communications: motives, objectives, and plans are hidden.

12. The search for improved working methods is encouraged and my ideas are listened to.

We just continue in the same old way with no change to working methods.

13. There is job commitment from my section; everyone's knowledge and skills are used to create a team identity.

Individuals in my section are left to their own devices; their knowledge and skills are not being fully used.

14. I seldom have time to wonder what to do next.

Work planning lacks organization; I find I have "slack" periods during the day.

15. Work relationships are designed in such a way that I feel I am able to make a positive contribution to the department because my voice will be heard.

Work relationships are based on organizational tradition: instruction is given and no questions are expected. I feel inhibited by this approach.

16. Individual development needs are understood and taken into account.

Individual development needs are dealt with on a "hit or miss" basis.

17. I feel stimulated by what I am doing and achieving.

I feel discouraged and frustrated by a lack of achievement.

82

18. We work hard because we have a common sense of purpose, and not because we are driven. | We are guided more by pressure from above than by a sense of commitment.

19. It is a very flexible staff; movement between sections is the norm. | We tend to operate in small, highly-structured sections.

20. The department accepts that conflicts sometimes arise, and attempts to find solutions that have the majority's agreement and understanding. | The department's leaders do not accept that conflicts arise; they let problems go unresolved, hoping they will disappear.

83

Thinking about your organization, read the following paired statements and put a check (✓) at the point on the scale corresponding most closely to the situation as you see it.

1 2 3 4 5 6

1. I am given feedback about my job performance and advice on how to improve it.

I am not given the opportunity to voice difficulties about my job and I am not informed sufficiently about my performance.

2. Decision-making is carried out by consultation throughout this organization.

Decision-making involves only the few people in authority in this organization.

3. My job is clearly defined and I understand what I am expected to do.

My job overlaps with others, and I am not clear about what I have to do.

4. Work is planned so that time schedules can be met.

Work planning is haphazard, and sometimes deadlines don't get met.

5. Organizational objectives are clearly defined.

I do not have a clear idea of this organization's aims and objectives.

6. I have a clear understanding of the goals of the other departments within the organization.

No one here knows exactly what other people are doing.

7. There is a well-defined chain of command here. I know who to take my problems to.

The chain of command is not well-defined; I am not clear who to take my problems to.

8. I feel I am encouraged to develop my potential and that I am making progress.

I feel I am not encouraged to develop my potential, and consequently I am not making progress.

| | 1 | 2 | 3 | 4 | 5 | 6 |

9. The different departments within the organization work well together, achieving a high standard of effectiveness.

There is considerable friction and lack of cooperation between different departments in the organization and we are not achieving a high standard of effectiveness.

10. I am able to use my own initiative to achieve results when tackling the duties of my job.

I work within the constraints of predetermined procedures to achieve results.

11. OPEN communications: motives, objectives, and plans are discussed openly.

CLOSED communications: motives, objectives, and plans are hidden.

12. The search for improved working methods is encouraged and my ideas are listened to.

We just continue in the same old way with no change to working methods.

13. There is commitment from my department to the work; everyone's knowledge and skills are being used to create a team identity.

Individuals in my department are left to their own devices; their knowledge and skills are not being fully used.

14. I seldom have time to wonder what to do next.

Work planning lacks organization; I find I have "slack" periods during the day.

15. Work relationships are designed in such a way that I feel I am able to make a positive contribution to the organization because my voice will be heard.

Work relationships are based on organizational tradition: instruction is given and no questions are expected. I feel inhibited by this approach.

16. Individual development needs are understood and taken into account.

Individual development needs are dealt with on a "hit or miss" basis.

17. I feel stimulated by what I am doing and achieving.

I feel discouraged and frustrated by a lack of achievement.

85

| | 1 | 2 | 3 | 4 | 5 | 6 | |

18. We work hard because we have a common sense of purpose and not because we are driven.

We are guided more by pressure from above than by a sense of commitment.

19. It is a very flexible staff; movement between departments is the norm.

We tend to operate in small, highly-structured departments.

20. The organization's leaders accept that conflicts sometimes arise, and attempt to find solutions that have the majority's agreement and understanding.

The organization's leaders do not accept that conflicts arise, and let problems go unresolved, hoping they will disappear.

86

Reproduced from *Training Needs Analysis—Second Edition*, Sharon Bartram and Brenda Gibson, HRD Press.

Survey analysis
Total number of people in the survey: _____

Paired statement number	Number of people choosing a rating of:						Additional comments
	1	2	3	4	5	6	
Job satisfaction 1.							
3.							
8.							
10.							
16.							
17.							
18							
Authority 2.							
7.							
15.							
Work planning 4.							
5.							
6.							
14.							
Communications 9.							
11.							
20.							
Work methods 12.							
13.							
19.							
Suggestions for improvements:							

8

What Drives This Organization?

Purpose
- To compare employee perceptions about what drives the organization, based on how employees are managed.
- To compare these perceptions with the views of senior managers.
- To suggest changes in management style in order to communicate a clear, consistent message about what drives the organization.

Description
This instrument uses a grid technique to compare driving forces of the organization and to identify the priorities within them.

Materials
1. Sufficient copies of documents 8.1 and 8.2.
2. A meeting room.

Collecting information

Methods	Benefits	Potential problems
Postal survey to: — all employees; — random sample; — peer-group sample; — mixed-levels sample.	— Easy to administer. — Generates information quickly.	— Low response rate. — Unable to check understanding.

Methods	Benefits	Potential problems
Completed individually, followed by group discussion with: — all employees; — random sample; — peer-group sample; — mixed-levels sample.	— Ensures high response rate. — Able to confirm understanding.	— Time

Methods

Postal survey
1. Brief the target group on the purpose of the instrument, stressing that feedback will be given about the outcomes.
2. Distribute copies of document 8.1 and agree to a schedule for completion and return.
3. At the same time, ask senior managers to complete the grid (document 8.1) before meeting to discuss findings.
4. Analyze the returned grids using document 8.2. Prepare the findings by using a tally system to record the number of times the options are given top priority, and list the range of scores within each option.
5. Arrange for a meeting with senior managers to present the findings and compare them to their own completed grids.
6. This meeting should highlight areas of agreement, discrepancies, and any unclear perceptions of what priorities are driving the organization.
7. Conclude the meeting by agreeing on action plans.

Completed individually followed by group discussion
1. Brief the target group on the purpose of the instrument, stressing that feedback will be given about the outcomes.
2. Distribute copies of document 8.1 and agree on a time schedule for a series of group discussion meetings. Allow up to 30 minutes per meeting. During the meetings, check that each person has completed the grid and answer questions. Collect the completed grids.
3. At the same time, ask senior managers to complete the grid (document 8.1) prior to meeting to discuss findings.

Follow steps 4 to 7 as above.

Analyzing results

Analysis type: NUMERICAL

Action
You will have carried out a frequency count on document 8.2 to determine the priorities of the organization, as perceived by the participants. Record the range of scores, also on document 8.2, and calculate averages so that you can compare the options.

The grid below suggests twelve options. The format of the grid allows you to compare the priority of each option against all the others. Follow these steps:

1. Take the first option across, STABILITY, and compare it with the different options down.
2. If you feel that STABILITY is of higher priority in your organization than CUSTOMER, put an "A" in the box. If CUSTOMER is the higher priority, put a "D" in the box.
3. Go along the row, each time deciding whether STABILITY is higher or lower in priority and putting an "A" or "D" in the boxes.
4. Repeat the process for CUSTOMER, going across the row and comparing it with all the other options.
5. Repeat for all the other options across, comparing them with all the options down.
6. When this is complete, add up the total number of "A"s allocated to each option across and put the score in the Total "A"s column. Now look down each column and record the total number of "D"s for each option.
7. Your grid is now complete. You will be able to see what you believe is really driving your organization: It will be the option that has scored the most when you add up the A and D totals.

Down

Option	STABILITY	CUSTOMER	INNOVATION	COMMUNITY	POWER	PROFIT	EXPANSION	PEOPLE	QUALITY	SALES	COSTS	PRODUCT	Total "A"s
STABILITY													
CUSTOMER													
INNOVATION													
COMMUNITY													
POWER													
PROFIT													
EXPANSION													
PEOPLE													
QUALITY													
SALES													
COSTS													
PRODUCT													
Total "D"s													

Across

92

Priority grid summary
Total number of respondents: _____

Option	Number of times identified as top priority
STABILITY	
CUSTOMER	
INNOVATION	
COMMUNITY	
POWER	
PROFIT	
EXPANSION	
PEOPLE	
QUALITY	
SALES	
COSTS	
PRODUCT	

Range within each option

Options

	STABILITY	CUSTOMER	INNOVATION	COMMUNITY	POWER	PROFIT	EXPANSION	PEOPLE	QUALITY	SALES	COSTS	PRODUCT
Range of scores												
Totals												

93

Reproduced from *Training Needs Analysis—Second Edition*,
Sharon Bartram and Brenda Gibson, HRD Press.

9
Evidence of Equality

Purpose
- To research the organization's approach to equality.
- To gather evidence indicating the positive or negative actions that affect equality within the organization.

Description
This instrument is an evidence-gathering exercise on issues relating to equality.

Materials
1. Documents 9.1 and 9.2 for reference.
2. Document 9.3.

Collecting information

Methods	Benefits	Potential problems
Personally gather examples of evidence for analysis and presentation.	— Objective information gathered.	— Access to information.

Method

Personally gather examples of evidence for analysis and presentation

1. Plan your approach to gathering evidence. Document 9.1 describes the type of evidence relevant to each issue.
2. Gather the information available in your organization.
3. Analyze the evidence you find and categorize it into examples of positive or negative actions. Use document 9.2 "Testing the Evidence" as your reference, and summarize your findings on document 9.3.
4. Arrange a meeting with senior managers to present your findings and come to agreement on action.

Analyzing results

Analysis type: COMBINATION

Action

The instrument suggests a method for reporting your results to participants, using document 9.3. To gather the evidence for this summary, use both content and numerical analysis. For example, when you are working with statistics, use frequency counts and calculate averages and comparisons to identify trends and priorities. With more descriptive material, use matrices to identify themes.

Issue	Relevant evidence
Promotion	Statistics showing comparisons of who is promoted (male/female; race; age; disability). Organization's written policy on access to training and development. Description of evaluation and rating process, with examples of documentation. Records of reviews from each department. Content of training and reviews. Examples of notices showing internal vacancies.
Stereotypes	Statistics showing comparisons of who does particular types of work (for example: clerical/managerial; full-time/part-time; manual/technical). Recruitment policy and the criteria used to select people for jobs.
Harassment	Records of complaints made and action taken. Records of interpersonal skills training throughout the organization. Content of interpersonal skills training.
Status	Statistics showing comparisons of who does particular types of work (for example: clerical/managerial; full-time/part-time; manual/technical). Comparison of perks and benefits available between jobs/job grades.
Selection	Recruitment policy and the criteria used to select people for jobs. Examples of vacancy advertisements and the range of outlets where they are placed. Records of recruitment training throughout the organization. Content of recruitment training.
Language	Examples of organizational communications (for example: newsletters, reports, etc.). Comparison of job titles. Records of language training made available. Content of language training. Examples of vacancy advertisements.
Work hours	Time sheets or time cards. Written terms and conditions.
Pay	Statistical comparisons between: male/female; full-time/part-time; different races; age ranges; disabilities.
Sick leave policy	Description of what is available and eligibility requirements.
Training and development	Training and policy eligibility requirements. Comparison of training available for different jobs; job grades; full-time/part-time employees. Examples of methods used to identify training needs. Content of training programs. Range of training methods used: courses; coaching; independent study, and so on. Ease of access to training: venue; times; dates.
Education	Education policy and eligibility requirements. Comparison of education benefits available to different employees: male/female; full-time/part-time; different races; age ranges; disabilities.
Goals	Description of how performance review is performed (with examples of documentation). Records of reviews. Content of performance reviews, meetings. Methods for identifying individual employee potential. Eligibility criteria for special programs.
Roadblocks and barriers	Examples of eligibility for promotion, training, education, and so on. Personal experiences of individuals.

Issue	Relevant evidence
Socializing	Examples of networking. Description of organization events.
Customers' perceptions, actual and perceived	Examples of range of customers. Personal experiences of individuals.
Role models	Personal experiences of individuals.
History	Background (within the organization). Organization records.
Influences	Description of location of organization. Background information about the local community. Examples of media influence inside the organization: periodicals; newspapers; radio; television; training materials used; and so on. Art and other visual displays showing positive/negative images of minority groups.
Hierarchies	Organization charts.

Testing the evidence

For each piece of evidence you gather, ask yourself these three questions:

1. Does the evidence show equal treatment?

    In other words, do all employees throughout the organization have equal opportunity and access based on knowledge and skills?

    For example: You would know that everyone was treated equally if you were called into a meeting and you were unable to predict the make-up of the group in attendance in terms of race, color, gender, sexual orientation, disability, age, and so on.

2. Does the evidence show direct discrimination?

    In other words, are some people treated less favorably than others because of race, color, ethnic or national origin, gender, sexual orientation, marital status, disability, or age?

    An example of direct discrimination: A college uses a pre-selection process, which automatically ensures that white male candidates are selected for interviews, while non-white female candidates are not—irrespective of any other criteria.

3. Does the evidence show indirect discrimination?

    In other words, are there any rules, requirements, or conditions that are equally applied to all but that have a disproportionate adverse impact on some and cannot be justified as reasonable or necessary on employment-related grounds?

    An example of indirect discrimination: A company recruiting camera technicians stipulates that candidates must have a degree in physics, even though this is not necessary to perform the job. (This requirement has a disproportionately adverse impact on women, who are less likely to have a physics degree than men.)

Reproduced from *Training Needs Analysis—Second Edition,*
Sharon Bartram and Brenda Gibson, HRD Press.

Evidence	Describe the ways in which the evidence shows:			Action
	Equal treatment	Direct discrimination	Indirect discrimination	

10

Is This a Learning Organization?

Purpose
To generate information about employee perceptions regarding the commitment of the organization to training and development.

Description
This instrument uses structured discussions to elicit information. Separate discussion sheets are available for people at different levels within the organization.

Materials
1. Sufficient copies of documents 10.1a–10.1e.
2. A meeting room.
3. Table E (p. 33) for analysis.
4. Document 10.2 for analysis.

Collecting information

Methods	Benefits	Potential problems
Individual interviews with people at different levels of the organization.	— All views taken into account. — Thorough analysis of the situation.	— Numbers included. — Time-consuming.
Group discussions with peer groups.	— Speeds up information gathering.	— Dominant views stifle other contributions. — Need enough time to assemble people.

Methods

Individual interviews with people at different levels of the organization
1. Decide whether to include all employees or a representative sample.
2. Brief the target group on the purpose of the instrument.
3. Arrange individual meetings, allowing up to one hour for each.
4. Select the appropriate document discussion sheet (10.1a–10.1e) according to the employee's level within the organization. During the meetings, use the worksheet to encourage comment and to record the information generated.
5. Produce a summary of the information gathered from each job level. Circulate the summary to those involved for comment and agreement.
6. Produce a report using the key points from each summary to provide information about the whole organization.
7. Discuss this report with senior managers and identify action points.

Group discussions with peer groups
Follow steps 1 and 2 above.
Then:
3. Arrange group meetings of not more than 12 people. Allow at least 90 minutes per meeting.

Follow steps 4 to 7 above.

Analyzing results

Analysis type: COMBINATION

Action
To help you analyze the large amount of information this instrument might generate, consider doing the following:

- Photocopy the questionnaires so that they are single-sided sheets when you give them to the participants.
- Color-code the questionnaires to distinguish between the different levels of participants.
- Organize the replies to each question by theme, perhaps cutting answers into separate strips of paper and sorting them.

Do an analysis of the answers to identify the main themes expressed by employees within the organization. Look for similar or different themes within a response group and across different levels within the organization. Use Table E for this purpose.

The questions can imply a way of working that leads toward a learning organization. Numerical analysis will show how many people hold similar views about the implied way of working and at what level. Use document 10.2 to carry out a frequency count.

Is this a learning organization?

Document 10.1a

Senior managers/decision-makers

QUESTIONS	KEY POINTS
1. What connection do you see between the organization's business plan and training and development?	
2. Is training and development viewed as an investment, or a cost?	
3. How is the budget for training and development decided upon?	
4. How much is budgeted?	
5. How is the budget usually spent?	
6. How much responsibility do managers have for managing this budget?	
7. What are your expectations of your managers and employees in general?	
8. How do you communicate these expectations to the people concerned?	
9. How do you make sure that people are meeting your expectations?	
10. What happens when people *do* meet your expectations?	

Reproduced from *Training Needs Analysis—Second Edition*, Sharon Bartram and Brenda Gibson, HRD Press.

QUESTIONS	KEY POINTS
11. What happens when people do not meet your expectations?	
12. What will your department look like in five years' time?	
13. What knowledge and skill will be needed . . . —at your level? —at other levels?	
14. Which of these do you already possess . . . —at your level? —at other levels?	
15. Which of these will need to be developed . . . —at your level? —at other levels?	
16. How do you identify potential?	
17. How do you prepare people for change?	
18. What types of learning opportunities do you offer? —external courses —in-house courses —special projects —on-the-job coaching	
19. What are the priorities in training and development for the next twelve months?	
20. Why are they priorities?	

Is this a learning organization?

Document 10.1b

Managers managing other managers

QUESTIONS	KEY POINTS
1. What connection do you see between the departmental objectives and training and development?	
2. Is training and development viewed as an investment, or a cost?	
3. How realistic is the budget for training and development?	
4. How much have you spent on training and development in the past 12 months?	
5. How was this spent?	
6. What analysis do you carry out to help you decide what kind of training and development is needed?	
7. What are your expectations of your managers and departmental employees?	
8. How do you communicate these expectations to the people concerned?	
9. How do you make sure that people are meeting your expectations?	
10. What happens when people achieve your expectations?	

105

Reproduced from *Training Needs Analysis—Second Edition,*
Sharon Bartram and Brenda Gibson, HRD Press.

QUESTIONS	KEY POINTS
11. What happens when people do not meet your expectations?	
12. What will your department look like in five years' time?	
13. What knowledge and skill will be needed . . . —at your level? —at other levels?	
14. Which of these do you already possess . . . —at your level? —at other levels?	
15. Which of these will need to be developed . . . —at your level? —at other levels?	
16. How do you identify potential?	
17. How do you prepare people for change?	
18. What types of learning opportunities do you offer? —external courses —in-house courses —special projects —on-the-job coaching	
19. What are the priorities in training and development for the next twelve months?	
20. Why are they priorities?	

Is this a learning organization?

Managers managing supervisors, or the equivalent

QUESTIONS	KEY POINTS
1. What connection do you see between the departmental objectives and training and development?	
2. Is training and development viewed as an investment, or a cost?	
3. How much authority do you have in recommending expenditures in training and development?	
4. What type of training and development have you arranged the past 12 months . . . —for yourself? —for your employees?	
5. What indicators do you use to assess the results of this training and development?	
6. What analysis do you carry out to help you decide what kind of training and development is needed?	
7. What are your expectations of your employees?	
8. How do you communicate these expectations to the people concerned?	
9. How do you make sure that people are meeting your expectations?	
10. What happens when people *do* meet your expectations?	

107

QUESTIONS	KEY POINTS
11. What happens when people do not meet your expectations?	
12. What will your department look like in five years' time?	
13. What knowledge and skill will be needed . . . —at your level? —at other levels?	
14. Which of these do you already possess . . . —at your level? —at other levels?	
15. Which of these will need to be developed . . . —at your level? —at other levels?	
16. How do you identify potential?	
17. How do you prepare people for change?	
18. What types of learning opportunities do you offer? —external courses —in-house courses —special projects —on-the-job coaching	
19. What are the priorities in training and development for the next twelve months?	
20. Why are they priorities?	

108

Reproduced from *Training Needs Analysis—Second Edition*, Sharon Bartram and Brenda Gibson, HRD Press.

First-line managers/supervisors or the equivalent

QUESTIONS	KEY POINTS
1. What connection do you see between your objectives and training and development?	
2. Is training and development viewed as an investment, or a cost?	
3. How much authority do you have in recommending expenditures for training and development?	
4. What type of training and development have you arranged in the past 12 months?	
5. What indicators do you use to check the results of this training and development?	
6. What analysis do you carry out to help you decide what kind of training and development is needed?	
7. What are your expectations of your employees?	
8. How do you communicate these expectations to the people concerned?	
9. How do you make sure that people are meeting your expectations?	
10. What happens when people *do* meet your expectations?	

109

Reproduced from *Training Needs Analysis—Second Edition,*
Sharon Bartram and Brenda Gibson, HRD Press.

QUESTIONS	KEY POINTS
11. What happens when people do not meet your expectations?	
12. What will your department look like in five years' time?	
13. What knowledge and skill will be needed . . . —at your level? —at other levels?	
14. Which of these do you already possess . . . —at your level? —at other levels?	
15. Which of these will need to be developed . . . —at your level? —at other levels?	
16. What is your role in identifying potential?	
17. How do you prepare people for change?	
18. How much of your time is spent coaching people on-the-job?	
19. What are your priorities in training and development for the next twelve months?	
20. Why are they priorities?	

Other employee grades

QUESTIONS	KEY POINTS
1. What training and development have you had in the last 12 months?	
2. Who carried out this training?	
3. What follow-up has there been?	
4. Is training and development viewed as an investment, or a cost?	
5. What involvement do you have in deciding what kind of training and development is made available to you?	
6. Are your skills being used in your current job?	
7. What skills do you have that could be utilized more effectively?	
8. How do you know what is expected of you in your job?	
9. What happens if you meet these expectations?	
10. What happens if you do not meet these expectations?	

QUESTIONS	KEY POINTS
11. What will your department/ section look like in five years' time?	
12. What knowledge and skills will you need to do your job then?	
13. Which of these do you already have?	
14. Which of these will you need to develop?	
15. What changes have taken place in the recent past?	
16. How did you find out about these changes?	
17. In what ways did the organization prepare you for these changes?	
18. How much of your time is spent training other people?	
19 What are your priorities in training and development for the next twelve months?	
20. Why are they priorities?	

Reproduced from *Training Needs Analysis—Second Edition*, Sharon Bartram and Brenda Gibson, HRD Press.

Implied way of working	Total number of respondents	Number of respondents expressing views consistent with their job responsibilities
There is a connection between the organization's business plan and training and development.		
Training and development is an investment.		
Training and development has a budget.		
Allocations are based on identified needs and future requirements.		
Managers manage the training and development budget based on their training plans.		
Expectations are clearly defined and are communicated throughout the organization at all levels.		
Systems are in place to monitor performance; people receive positive feedback in recognition of their successful achievements, and constructive feedback so they can improve.		
There is a clear vision of where the organization is going.		
Systems for identifying knowledge and skill requirements are in place and kept up-to-date.		
Systems for identifying employee potential exist and people have the opportunity to develop their potential.		
People are communicated with and listened to when change is to take place.		
A wide range of learning opportunities are available to people.		
Priorities for training are clearly identified and related to improving or enhancing the way things are done.		

III
Managing Resources

This section shows you how to evaluate employee performance against best-practice standards. There are seven instruments:

11. Personal Assessment
12. Management Match
13. Managing Time
14. Managing People
15. Managing Expenditures
16. How Others See Me
17. How Do I See my Managers?

The target group is anyone who is responsible for managing company resources, and one of the most important resources in any organization is its people.

Personal Assessment helps company leaders determine how much time they devote to managing other people.

Management Match helps people discover their own management strengths and identify areas for development in managing themselves and others; this instrument also helps them review what they consider to be the organization's priorities.

Managing Time highlights the problems people have managing their time and helps them use it more effectively.

Managing People requires the respondents to describe their personal style and approach when managing others. This can then be compared with benchmarks to identify strengths and weaknesses.

Managing Expenditures measures current performance against best-practice criteria.

How Others See Me uses the powerful process of structured feedback from those who are managed, comparing it with how the managers see themselves.

How do I See my Managers? shows senior managers how to assess the competence of managers who report to them. Weaknesses are identified by matching certain management factors against actual performance.

Not all trainers are expected to be involved in managing a company's resources, so ask yourself if it is your responsibility. If it is not, move on to the next section. If it is, make sure that you have made the preparations necessary to the success of this aspect of training needs analysis. Using this checklist as your guide. Have you . . .

Preparation	Y	N	Action
. . . identified and won the support of the appropriate sponsor?			
. . . clarified your objectives? Do you know what you want to achieve by using the instrument?			
. . . assessed the potential problems of using the instruments in this target group and made contingencies for them?			
. . . considered the expectations that taking part will raise, and discussed them with your sponsor and other managers?			
. . . practiced your coaching skills, as required by a number of the instruments? They are: —listening —questioning —seeking contributions —building on proposals			

116

Preparation	Y	N	Action
. . . made sure you know and understand the best responses to the instruments?			
. . . selected the best method of collecting the information from the options given in the instrument?			
. . . prepared your briefing for the target group?			

11
Personal Assessment

Purpose
To find out how much time is spent carrying out key management activities, and to assess performance in achieving the desired results. Analyzing this information will help determine where training is necessary to meet organizational, departmental, and personal objectives.

Description
This instrument uses an activity log and an analysis sheet to collect information.

Materials
1. Sufficient copies of documents 11.1 and 11.2.

Collecting information

Methods	*Benefits*	*Potential problems*
Activity log completed individually, followed by interview to complete the analysis.	— Easy to administer. — Creates ownership in the user. — Minimal intrusion into user's routine.	— Analysis might be time-consuming.
Activity log and analysis completed individually, followed by interview to discuss the findings.	— Easy to administer. — Gives the user total control. — Developmental activity in itself.	— Level of commitment required by the user.

Methods

Activity log completed individually, followed by interview to complete the analysis

1. Brief the target group on the purpose of the instrument.
2. Give each person sufficient copies of the activity log (document 11.1) to generate a useful amount of information, and agree on a deadline for completion.
3. Arrange and carry out interviews with each person, using document 11.2 as the basis for the discussion. At the end of the interview, you should have completed document 11.2, which summarizes the person's training needs. Allow at least 90 minutes per interview.

Activity log and analysis completed individually, followed by interview to discuss the findings

1. Brief the target group on the purpose of the instrument.
2. Give each person sufficient copies of the activity log (document 11.1) to generate a useful amount of information, and a copy of document 11.2 to analyze the findings. Agree on a deadline for completion.
3. Arrange and carry out interviews with each person, using document 11.2 as the basis for the discussion. At the end of the interview, you should have found out enough information from the person to confirm their training needs. Allow at least one hour per interview.

Analyzing results

Analysis type: NUMERICAL

Action

This instrument focuses on comparisons.

Whichever option you choose, use the analysis document to identify those responsibilities or activities that the person carries out often, but that can be improved. These are likely to be priority training needs. The next level of priority will be those responsibilities that the person only occasionally carries out, but areas where they believe they could use some improvement. Look at the responsibilities the person carries out only occasionally or never (but which are an important part of managing effectively), and then draw up a personal development plan for future action.

Activity log

Use this sheet to record the responsibilities you carry out during your workday. To find out how much time you are spending on these activities, make a mark to represent each fifteen-minute period spent on the activity that best describes what you are doing. At the end of each day, total up the number of marks against each activity and convert this into real time.

Activity	Day one	Day two	Day three	Day four	Day five
Maintaining and improving the quality of what we do					
Instigating change in the way things are done					
Controlling resources other than people					
Recruiting and selecting staff					
Developing people, including self					
Allocating tasks and monitoring results					
Developing effective working relationships					
Dealing with information					
Solving problems and making decisions					
Other (please specify)					
Total					

121

Use the information from your log to indicate how often you do each of these things and rate your performance. Select Often, Occasionally, or Never to indicate frequency. Select a performance rating of X for *excellent*, C for *competent*, or D for *needs developing*. You should have two checks (✓) for each activity.

Activity	Often	Occasionally	Never	X	C	D
Maintaining and improving the quality of what we do						
Instigating change in the way things are done						
Controlling resources other than people						
Recruiting and selecting staff						
Developing people, including self						
Allocating tasks and monitoring results						
Developing effective working relationships						
Dealing with information						
Solving problems and making decisions						
Other (please specify)						

12
Management Match

Purpose
- To discover strengths and areas for improvement in ten managerial and supervisory activities.
- To compare the needs of the organization with the skills of its managers and supervisors.
- To develop training plans for individuals and groups.

Description
This instrument uses a card sort approach to extract information.

Materials
1. Sufficient supply of documents 12.1a–e, each taped or glued onto a card and then cut and organized into packs.
2. Sufficient copies of document 12.2.
3. Findings sheet (document 12.3).
4. A meeting room.

Collecting information

Methods	Benefits	Potential problems
Group activity with a mix of seniority levels.	— Clearer picture of organization-wide training needs. — Sharing of perceptions about what is important to the organization.	— Difficult to arrange. — Fear of disclosure.

Methods	Benefits	Potential problems
Group activity on a departmental basis.	— Clearer picture of departmental training needs.	— Fear of disclosure. — Disruption to work routines.
Group activity with similar levels of seniority across all areas.	— Able to target training more accurately.	— Fear of disclosure. — Availability of individuals.
Individual structured interviews.	— Identifies specific training needs and individuals with potential. — Non-threatening. — Limits disruption to work.	— Time-consuming.
Separate structured interviews with individuals and their managers, followed by joint discussion.	— Opportunity to give and receive feedback on performance. — Wins the commitment of the manager to the training plan. — Identifies specific training needs, and individuals who have potential.	— Time-consuming. — Overlap with an evaluation or appraisal procedure that might be in use.

Methods

Group activity (first three methods)

1. Brief the target group on the purpose of the instrument.
2. Hold a meeting with the group, allowing at least two hours.
3. Give each person a pack of cards cut up from document 12.1a–e and a copy of document 12.2, their personal assessment sheet. Allow sufficient time for each person to sort the cards and record their responses.
4. Leave one pack of cards with the group and collect the rest.
5. Ask the group to agree on the top ten priorities for the organization and to record their selections onto their own personal assessment sheet (document 12.2).
6. Allow sufficient time for each person to reflect on their personal strengths and areas for improvement (matching these with the priorities for the organization), and to write how they can best use and enhance their abilities on their personal assessment sheet (document 12.2).
7. Make a copy of each completed document 12.2 and explain that they will be used to compile an overall findings sheet in order to identify the priority training needs of the group and to form the basis for feedback.

Individual structured interviews

1. Brief the target group on the purpose of the instrument.
2. Arrange separate interviews with each person, allowing approximately one hour per interview.
3. Give each person a pack of cards cut up from document 12.1a–e and ask them to arrange the cards into three piles: their top ten strengths in priority order; their top ten areas for improvement in priority order; and a pile to be discarded.
4. Record their choices onto a personal assessment sheet (document 12.2).
5. Reshuffle the pack of cards and ask the person to arrange two piles: the top ten areas of most importance to the organization, in priority order; and a pile to be discarded.
6. Record their choices on a personal assessment sheet (document 12.2) and discuss them. Ask participants to comment on how their capabilities can be utilized and enhanced. Record their comments onto document 12.2.
7. Give a copy of the completed document 12.2 to the person and explain that the overall findings will form the basis of feedback about training plans.

Separate structured interviews with individuals and their managers, followed by joint discussion

Follow steps 1 to 6 as described for the individual structured interviews.
Then:

7. Repeat these steps with the individual's manager, asking the manager to prioritize the strengths and weaknesses of the employee as the manager sees them.
8. Arrange a meeting with the individual, their manager, and yourself to discuss the findings and agree on the training needs to be addressed.

Analyzing results

Analysis type: NUMERICAL

Action

Complete a frequency count, using document 12.3 to summarize the initial findings—that is, the times a card has been selected as a top priority for the organization, a "top ten" strength, and a "top ten" improvement need. By comparing those items selected most often as organizational top priorities, find the relationship between the priorities and whether the respondents see each one more as a strength or weakness that can be improved. Note down on document 12.3 whether or not the relationship suggests a training need. Once you begin to see how many people have a particular training need, you can consider your options to meet that need and complete document 12.3.

Experience suggests that respondents do not fall neatly into categories. You may also compare those aspects that respondents regard as strengths but not priorities for the organization. Are any actions necessary to utilize these abilities fully? Similarly, with items selected as improvement needs but not priorities, you can discuss these needs and decide on appropriate actions.

Motivation

1. Encouraging the members of my team to take a real interest in their jobs.
2. Encouraging good work and discouraging bad.
3. Dealing with the individual who has the ability but does not do a good job.
4. Persuading my team to use initiative—to see what has to be done and do it without being told.

Delegation

5. Knowing what to do myself and knowing what to delegate to others.
6. Dealing with individuals who want to take on more responsibility (which I know they can't handle).
7. Dealing with individuals who could take on more responsibility but do not want it.
8. Allowing my team to make decisions regarding what to do and how to do it.

Dealing with problems

9. Choosing the best of several alternative ways of doing a job.
10. Identifying the real problem in a difficult situation.
11. Organizing a complicated problem into manageable tasks.
12. Making decisions when necessary.

Training

13. Assessing whether the members of my team know how to do their jobs.
14. Measuring the effects of the training my team receives to ensure that it is working.
15. Training my team using a logical step-by-step approach.
16. Identifying training needs of team members.

Performance

17. Setting achievable standards for myself and others.
18. Evaluating my own and others' performance fairly.
19. Correcting poor performance promptly and effectively.
20. Helping others with personal problems that affect their job performance.

Planning

21. Planning the work of my team.
22. Monitoring work progress against the plan.
23. Anticipating problems that might interfere with the work's progress.
24. Using the resources of my team effectively by assigning work appropriately to individuals.

127

Reproduced from *Training Needs Analysis—Second Edition,*
Sharon Bartram and Brenda Gibson, HRD Press.

Time

25. Coaching my team to make better use of time.
26. Dealing with the excessive demands placed upon my time by other people.
27. Using my time each day effectively.
28. Keeping my demands on other people's time to a level appropriate for the job.

Ideas

29. Generating suggestions from my team.
30. Handling poor or bad suggestions from others in a way that does not discourage them.
31. Encouraging my team's commitment and cooperation regarding new ways of doing things.
32. Selling new ideas to my manager.

Teamwork

33. Helping the individuals in my area to work effectively together as a team.
34. Dealing with conflict between individuals whose personalities clash.
35. Dealing with individuals who don't take their share of the load.
36. Ensuring effective relations between my team and others so that we work smoothly together.

Communication

37. Communicating clearly what I expect from my team.
38. Giving instructions to others to achieve the results I want.
39. Creating effective communications with my manager.
40. Running effective meetings with others.

1. Encouraging my team to take a real interest in their jobs.	2. Encouraging good work and discouraging bad.
3. Dealing with the individual who has the ability but does not do a good job.	4. Persuading my team to use initiative—to see what has to be done and do it without being told.
5. Knowing what to do myself and knowing what to delegate to others.	6. Dealing with individuals who are anxious to take on more responsibility (which I know they can't handle).
7. Dealing with individuals who could take more responsibility but who don't want it.	8. Allowing my team to make decisions regarding what to do and how to do it.

Reproduced from *Training Needs Analysis—Second Edition*,
Sharon Bartram and Brenda Gibson, HRD Press.

Document 12.1b

9. Choosing the best of several alternative ways of doing a job.	10. Identifying the real problem in a difficult situation.
11. Organizing a complicated problem into manageable tasks.	12. Making decisions when necessary.
13. Assessing whether the members of my team know how to do their jobs.	14. Measuring the effects of the training my team receives to ensure that it is working.
15. Training my team using a logical step-by-step approach.	16. Identifying the training needs of my team members.

130

Reproduced from *Training Needs Analysis—Second Edition,* Sharon Bartram and Brenda Gibson, HRD Press.

17. Setting achievable standards for myself and others.	18. Evaluating my own and others' performance fairly.
19. Correcting poor performance promptly and effectively.	20. Helping others with personal problems that affect their job performance.
21. Planning the work of my team.	22. Monitoring work progress against the plan.
23. Anticipating problems that might interfere with the work's progress.	24. Using the resources of my team effectively by assigning work appropriately to individuals.

25. Coaching my team to make better use of time.	26. Dealing with the excessive demands placed upon my time by other people.
27. Using my time each day effectively.	28. Keeping my demands on other people's time to a level appropriate for the job.
29. Generating suggestions from my team.	30. Handling poor or bad suggestions from others in a way that does not discourage them.
31. Encouraging my team's commitment and cooperation regarding new ways of doing things.	32. Selling new ideas to my manager.

33. Helping the individuals in my area to work effectively together as a team.	34. Dealing with conflict between individuals whose personalities clash.
35. Dealing with individuals who don't take their share of the load.	36. Ensuring effective relations between my team and others so that we work smoothly together.
37. Communicating clearly what I expect from my team.	38. Giving instructions to others to achieve the results I want.
39. Creating effective communications with my manager.	40. Running effective meetings with others.

133

My top ten strengths are:	My top ten areas for improvement are:	The top ten priorities for the organization are:
1.	1.	1.
2.	2.	2.
3.	3.	3.
4.	4.	4.
5.	5.	5.
6.	6.	6.
7.	7.	7.
8.	8.	8.
9.	9.	9.
10	10.	10.

Action:

Card number	Times selected as top ten priority for organization	Times selected as top ten strengths	Times selected as top ten improvement needs	Training need (yes/no)	Training options
Motivation 1.					
2.					
3.					
4.					
Delegation 5.					
6.					
7.					
8.					
Problems 9.					
10.					
11.					
12.					
Training 13.					
14.					
15.					
16.					
Performance 17.					
18.					
19.					
20.					

Card number	Times selected as top ten priority for organization	Times selected as top ten strengths	Times selected as top ten improvement needs	Training need (yes/no)	Training options
Planning 21.					
22.					
23.					
24.					
Time 25.					
26.					
27.					
28.					
Ideas 29.					
30.					
31.					
32.					
Teamwork 33.					
34.					
35.					
36.					
Communication 37.					
38.					
39.					
40.					

136

Reproduced from *Training Needs Analysis—Second Edition,*
Sharon Bartram and Brenda Gibson, HRD Press.

13

Managing Time

Purpose
- To identify aspects of self-organization requiring improvement in order to increase the effectiveness of the individual's job performance.
- To discover any underlying organizational issues that may be manifesting themselves as symptoms of poor time management.

Description
This instrument is a survey for individuals. It can be adapted into a card sort as an alternative method of gathering information.

Materials
1. Sufficient copies of document 13.1.
2. A meeting room.
3. Flip chart, paper and pens.
4. Document 13.2 for analysis.

Collecting information

Methods	Benefits	Potential problems
Survey completed individually, followed by individual interviews.	— Easy to administer. — Each person will have their own development plan.	— Misses the opportunity to identify trends. — Time-consuming to analyze.
Survey completed individually, followed by group discussions (either on a departmental basis or across departments).	— Easy to administer. — Trends will be identified.	— Some individuals' training needs may be missed. — Difficulty in bringing groups together.

Methods

Survey completed individually, followed by individual interviews

1. Brief the target group on the purpose of the instrument.
2. Give each person a copy of document 13.1 and agree on a deadline for completion.
3. Arrange an interview with each person, allowing up to one hour per interview.
4. Discuss the results of the survey and record the top five priorities.
5. Coach the individual to find ways of overcoming the problems.
6. Explain that their information will be the basis for an action plan in the form of a matrix showing trends and development needs.

Survey completed individually, followed by group discussions (either on a departmental basis or across departments)

Follow steps 1 and 2 above.

Then:

3. Arrange group discussions, allowing 90 minutes for each group.
4. Using a pre-prepared flip chart displaying the 20 statements, ask each person to place a red checkmark next to their most important statement and a black one next to their other four choices.
5. Encourage the group to analyze the findings, concentrating on how their jobs are affected and how the organization is affected.
6. Explain that their information will be the basis for an action plan in the form of a matrix to show trends and development needs.

Whichever method you choose, it will be helpful to explain that the statements on the survey fall into the following categories:

Category	*Statement(s)*
Personal disorganization	1, 2
Lack of discipline	3, 4, 5, 6
Lack of priorities	7, 8
Reading	9
Interruptions—telephone	10, 11
Interruptions—unexpected visitors	12, 13
Inability to say "no"	14, 15
Inability to finish work	16, 17
Indecision and delay	18, 19, 20

Analyzing results

Analysis type: NUMERICAL

Action
Responding positively to the statements indicates training needs in particular areas:

Statement number	Training need
1, 3, 4, 5, 16	Setting objectives and standards; monitoring results
2, 6, 7, 8, 9, 10, 11, 17	Setting priorities; planning
12, 13, 14, 15	Assertiveness
18, 19, 20	Decision-making

To identify the training needs, count the number of times a statement has been selected thusly:

- describing the respondents in the workplace
- not describing the respondents in the workplace
- one of the top five factors having the biggest impact on the respondents' jobs
- priority 1, 2, 3, 4, or 5.

Use document 13.2 for this purpose.
   Next identify the relationship between those statements that:

- appear most often as describing the respondents in the workplace
- appear most often in the top five factors
- are ranked as either 1, 2, or 3, in priority.

These statements are likely to reflect the most important training needs. A second level of needs will emerge from those statements most often describing respondents that appear in the top five factors ranked as either 4 or 5.

Please read each of the 20 statements and place a check (✓) in either the "yes" or "no" column if the statement describes you in your workplace.

		YES	NO
1.	I don't have a routine or system for organizing my time.		
2.	I have a fear of forgetting things.		
3.	I don't set performance standards.		
4.	I lack direction in my work.		
5.	I don't always follow up on work.		
6.	I tend to respond to urgent matters, postponing what is important.		
7.	I don't have time to plan.		
8.	I would rather be doing than thinking.		
9.	I have no priorities for what to read and how thoroughly to read it.		
10.	I tend to make unstructured telephone calls.		
11.	I don't prioritize, so all telephone calls are put through to me.		
12.	I don't discourage drop-in visitors.		
13.	I find it difficult to bring visits to a close.		
14.	I like to feel important and involved in everything.		
15.	I don't know how to say "no" and fear causing offense.		
16.	I lack an overview and perspective of my work.		
17.	I suffer from setting unrealistic time estimates and lack of deadlines.		
18.	I don't like making decisions for fear of what might happen if mistakes are made.		
19.	I don't always anticipate the effects of my decisions.		
20.	I suffer from an ineffective approach to making decisions.		

From the statements where you have checked "yes," select the top five that have the biggest impact on how effective you are in your job. Try to rank the five in order of importance:

Biggest impact   statement number:
                        statement number:
                        statement number:
                        statement number:
                        statement number:

Reproduced from *Training Needs Analysis—Second Edition*,
Sharon Bartram and Brenda Gibson, HRD Press.

Managing time

Document 13.2

Training needs and statements	Times selected as describing person in workplace (YES)	Times selected as not describing person in workplace (NO)	Times appearing in top 5	Times placed in priority:				
Setting objectives and standards; monitoring results				1	2	3	4	5
1. Lack of routine or system								
3. Lack of performance standards								
4. Lack of direction								
5. Lack of follow-up on work								
16. Lack of overview and perspective to work								
Setting priorities, planning								
2. Fear of forgetting things								
6. Responding to urgent matters, postponing important ones								
7. Lack of time to plan								
8. Rather be doing than thinking								
9. Lack of priorities for what to read								
10. Making unstructured telephone calls								
11. Lack of priorities, so all calls are put through to me								
17. Setting unrealistic time estimates; lack of deadlines								
Assertiveness								
12. Not discouraging drop-in visitors								
13. Difficulty in bringing visits to a close								
14. Need to feel important and involved in everything								
15. Not knowing how to say "no"; fear of causing offense								
Decision-making								
18. Dislike making decisions; fear of making mistakes								
19. Not anticipating effects of decisions								
20. Ineffective approach to decision-making								

141

14

Managing People

Purpose
- To help newly appointed managers develop management of their teams.
- To highlight the training needs of individuals in managing others before they are appointed as first-line managers.
- To assess the competence of individuals in managing others when they have received no previous formal training.

Description
This instrument consists of a series of open-ended statements that allow individuals to describe their ways of managing people. Replies are matched to a suggested check-list of benchmark responses. This benchmark system can be adapted to suit the organization.

Materials
1. Sufficient copies of document 14.1.
2. Document 14.2.
3. Documents 14.3 and 14.4 for analysis.

Collecting information

Methods	Benefits	Potential problems
Completed individually, followed by individual interviews.	— Each person will have a specific development plan. — Trends can be incorporated into training courses for groups of people. — Answers can be clarified.	— Time-consuming in analysis.

Methods	Benefits	Potential problems
Postal survey.	— Easy to administer. — Speeds up analysis.	— Percentage of surveys not returned. — Ambiguous answers not clarified.

Methods

Completed individually, followed by individual interviews
1. Brief the target group on the purpose of the instrument.
2. Give each person a copy of document 14.1 and agree on a time schedule for completion.
3. Arrange an interview with each person, allowing at least one hour per interview.
4. Discuss their responses, noting how near they match the benchmark checklist (document 14.2). Record gaps in knowledge as potential training needs.
5. Explain that the information in their responses will form the basis of an action plan. Make a copy of the completed document for further analysis.
6. Develop a matrix to show how each individual matches the benchmark checklist (document 14.2).

Postal survey
Follow steps 1, 2, 5, and 6 as above.

Analyzing results

Analysis type: CONTENT

Action
To develop personal action plans: Complete a matrix for each individual, using document 14.3. This is a variation on the template, Table E (p. 33), to match the needs of this instrument. In column A on the document, record the person's actual wording that you believe corresponds to the benchmark response. In column B, record those elements of the benchmark response that you believe were not covered by the person's response. In column C, describe the training needs that would enable the person to match the benchmark response in full.

Alternatively, ask the respondents to complete a matrix by comparing their own responses to the benchmarks. This increased involvement has the added benefit of enabling the respondents to identify their own training needs. They will be more committed to the training process.

Finally, summarize all the training needs identified from this content analysis using document 14.4.

Please complete the following sentences as fully as possible:

A. When deciding my future personnel requirements, the considerations I take into account are:

B. When selecting a new person as a member of my team, the factors I take into account are:

C. The ways in which I develop and improve the performance of my team are:

D. The steps I take to come up with appropriate activities to develop the individuals on my team are:

E. The ways in which I improve my own job performance are:

F.   When setting work objectives, the factors I take into account are:

G.   In order to achieve these objectives, I plan activities and determine work methods in the following way:

H.   The steps I take when allocating work are:

I.   The methods I use to measure the results achieved by my team, the individuals on the team, and myself are:

J.   To ensure that the performance feedback I provide is effective, I take these steps:

K.   To win and keep the trust and support of my staff, the steps I take are:

146

L. To win and keep the trust and support of my manager, the steps I take are:

M. To build relationships with work colleagues, the steps I take are:

N. To deal with interpersonal conflict, the methods I use are:

O. When using the discipline or grievance procedure, the factors I take into account are:

P. When a member of my team has a personal problem that is affecting their work, the steps I take are:

Sentence	Benchmark response
A.	Strengths and weaknesses of current team; Needs of the department and organization; Quantifiable information on current team (for example: age range, task coverage, succession plans); Legislation on equal opportunity policies; Financial constraints.
B.	Evidence from the prospective employee of skills appropriate to the requirements of the job; The organization's selection criteria; Legislation on sex discrimination and race relations; The balance of skills and qualities the prospective employee will bring to the existing team.
C.	Maintain up-to-date information on strengths and weaknesses of team members; Encourage individuals to set realistic objectives for themselves; Match individual talents to assignments; Provide opportunities for formal training; Use coaching as a way of developing people on a daily basis; Give regular constructive feedback on results achieved.
D.	Match individual talents to assignments; Encourage individuals to evaluate their own learning and development needs; Analyze activities to clarify the opportunities they present.
E.	Set achievable, realistic, and challenging objectives for myself; Review my performance with my manager regularly; Review my performance with my team regularly.
F.	The objectives can be achieved; The objectives do not clash with other commitments; Communicate clearly the objectives to those concerned and check understanding of what is expected; The methods used to monitor progress; Defining a mixture of short, medium, and long-term objectives.
G.	Assess the amount of supervision each individual will require; Seek contributions from individuals on how the objectives can be achieved; Ensure that the activities and work methods will provide development opportunities; Ensure that the activities and work methods are in line with the organization's way of working; Make the best use of available resources.
H.	Use the strengths of the team to best effect; Clearly define responsibilities and limits of authority; Provide individuals with learning opportunities; Clearly communicate expectations and check for understanding; Be available for ongoing guidance as requested by the team and individuals.
I.	Monitor progress and take appropriate actions (for example: praise good performance; give constructive feedback to improve performance); Define quantifiable measures (for example: quality; quantity; timescales) as part of objectives and note performance against these.

148

Sentence	Benchmark response
J.	Give detailed feedback that can be acted upon; Use observed examples, not opinions; Praise good performance and highlight areas for improvement; Give feedback at the appropriate time and place.
K.	Listen to the views of the team and individuals; Encourage contributions from the team and individuals; Keep the team and individuals regularly informed; Be consistent in praising good performance and highlighting areas for improvement; Carry out undertakings made to team and individuals; Give reasons if ideas and suggestions are not implemented
L.	Keep my manager regularly informed; Meet the standards expected of me; Seek information from my manager as appropriate; Do not allow disagreements to spoil the relationship; Present proposals for action supported by quantifiable justifications; Accept refusal of proposals by asking for reasons and amending proposals appropriately.
M.	Carry out promises and undertakings; Deal with differences of opinion in a way that maintains respect; Freely exchange opinions and information; Encourage open and honest behavior by setting a good example; Listen to colleagues.
N.	Clearly communicate the standards of work and behavior expected; Provide regular opportunities for people to discuss problems; Take prompt action to deal with potential and actual conflict.
O.	Ensure that my team members are kept informed of the procedures; Use the procedures at the appropriate times; Be impartial in applying the procedures; Take notes and record details when using the procedures.
P.	Find a private place to discuss the situation with the person; Listen and reflect the person's comments back so that they take responsibility for finding their own solutions; Monitor the situation to ensure a positive outcome.

Benchmark response	A What matches benchmark	B Aspects of benchmark not matched	C Potential training need
Sentence A Deciding personnel requirements			
Sentence B Selecting a new person			
Sentence C Develop and improve team performance			
Sentence D Discovering opportunities to develop individuals			
Sentence E Improving own job performance			
Sentence F Factors involved in setting objectives			
Sentence G Ways of planning and determining work methods			
Sentence H Allocating work			
Sentence I Methods for measuring team, individual, and personal results			
Sentence J Ensuring effective feedback to people			
Sentence K Steps to winning and keeping trust of staff			

Benchmark response	A What matches benchmark	B Aspects of benchmark not matched	C Potential training need
Sentence L Steps to winning and keeping trust of manager			
Sentence M Steps to building relationships with colleagues			
Sentence N Methods for dealing with interpersonal conflict			
Sentence O Factors involved in using grievance and discipline procedure			
Sentence P Steps when team member has personal problem			

Potential training needs	Names of respondents requiring training	Suggested action

15

Managing Expenditures

Purpose
- To identify ways of improving the processes and techniques used in managing expenditures.
- To discover the degree to which *best practice* standards are currently followed when managing expenditures.
- To determine specific expenditure techniques required by managers.

Description
This instrument is a survey that combines a series of statements describing *best practice* with a list of techniques useful in managing expenditures.

Materials
1. Sufficient copies of document 15.1.
2. One copy of document 15.2.
3. Meeting room.
4. Document 15.3 for analysis.

Collecting information

Methods	*Benefits*	*Potential problems*
Postal survey.	— Easy to administer. — Information generated quickly.	— Percentage of surveys not returned. — Unable to confirm understanding of respondents.
Individually completed, followed by individual interviews.	— Able to confirm understanding of participants.	— Time-consuming.

Methods	Benefits	Potential problems
Telephone survey.	— Speeds up information gathering. — Opportunity to check understanding. — Increases response rate.	— Might be interpreted as an impersonal approach. — Can be time-consuming if planned call times are not met.

Methods

Postal survey
1. Brief the target group on the purpose of the instrument.
2. Distribute one copy of the survey (document 15.1) to each person, asking them to make a copy of their responses before returning the completed survey.
3. Agree on a time schedule for completion.
4. Analyze the completed surveys using document 15.2 and report the findings back to the target group.

Individual interviews
1. Brief the target group on the purpose of the instrument.
2. Distribute one copy of the survey (document 15.1) to each person and agree on a time and date for the interview.
3. Allow at least 30 minutes per interview.
4. Take a copy of each completed survey and analyze them using document 15.2.
5. Report the findings back to the target group.

Telephone survey
1. Brief the target group on the purpose of the instrument, distributing a copy of document 15.1 to each person so they can consider their responses. Arrange a convenient time for your follow-up telephone call, allowing up to 20 minutes per call.
2. Have ready a copy of document 15.1 at the start of each call to record their responses.
3. Work through the statements, placing a check (✓) in the appropriate column on document 15.1.
4. Confirm the responses they have given.
5. Complete the call by asking which of the techniques they have selected to further assist them in managing expenditures. Read the list of techniques out loud and indicate the choices with a check (✓). Add any different techniques that they request.

6. Confirm the selections they have made, thank them for their cooperation, and explain that they will receive a copy of the findings once all the analysis has been completed.
7. Analyze the surveys using document 15.2 and report the findings to the target group.

Analyzing results

Analysis type: NUMERICAL

Action

By following the instructions given in the methods above, you will complete a frequency count and record your information on document 15.2.

To identify priorities, compare those statements selected most often as something that is done only "sometimes" or "never" and the consequences of this. Consequences can be:

- the impact on the person/department/organization if the action described in the statement is not happening
- the impact that training in this aspect might have on the person/department/ organization.

Note the consequences in the appropriate column on document 15.2.

You will also have completed a frequency count to identify those expenditure techniques that respondents would like to know more about. Display them in order of the number of times they have been selected, together with initial ideas on training options. Use document 15.3 for this purpose.

Please read the following statements carefully and then place a check (✓) to indicate whether you do this always, frequently, sometimes, or never.

Statements	Always	Frequently	Sometimes	Never
Budgeting expenditures:				
I gather information from internal and external sources to develop recommendations for expenditures.				
I seek contributions from the appropriate people to develop my recommendations.				
The benefits to be derived from the expenditure are clearly stated in my recommendations.				
I present my recommendations in a clear and concise way.				
I compare the actual expenditure with the recommendations to make improvements in the future.				
Controlling expenditures:				
I make sure that everyone on my team knows how they can contribute to controlling resources.				
I keep expenditures within agreed-upon budgets.				
I recognize when I have to refer requests for expenditures to other people, and act promptly.				
I keep accurate, legible, and complete records.				
When I see ways of increasing efficiency, I pass on my recommendations to the appropriate people quickly.				
I correctly interpret information about costs and the utilization of resources.				
I take corrective action promptly to minimize the effect of any deviations from expenditure plans.				

To assist me in managing expenditures, I would like to know more about the items indicated. (Place a check ✓ in the boxes provided to indicate your choices. Spaces have been left for you to add any techniques not mentioned in these lists.)

Trend analysis		Balance sheets		
Zero-based budgeting		Profit and loss		
Life-cycle budgeting		Value analysis		
Depreciation		Break-even analysis		
Cash flow		Cost-benefit analysis		

Reproduced from *Training Needs Analysis—Second Edition*,
Sharon Bartram and Brenda Gibson, HRD Press.

Statements	No. of times always selected	No. of times frequently selected	No. of times sometimes selected	No. of times never selected	Consequences
Budgeting expenditures:					
I gather information from internal and external sources to develop recommendations for expenditures.					
I seek contributions from the appropriate people to develop my recommendations.					
The benefits to be derived from the expenditure are clearly stated in my recommendations.					
I present my recommendations in a clear and concise way.					
I compare the actual expenditure with the recommendations to make improvements in the future.					
Controlling expenditures:					
I make sure that everyone on my team knows how they can contribute to controlling resources.					
I keep expenditures within agreed-upon budgets.					
I recognize when I have to refer requests for expenditures to other people, and act promptly.					
I keep accurate, legible, and complete records.					
When I see ways of increasing efficiency, I pass on my recommendations to the appropriate people quickly.					
I correctly interpret information about costs and the utilization of resources.					
I take corrective action promptly to minimize the effect of any deviations from expenditure plans.					

Technique	No. of times selected	Technique	No. of times selected	Technique	No. of times selected
Trend analysis		Balance sheets			
Zero-based budgeting		Profit and loss			
Life-cycle budgeting		Value analysis			
Depreciation		Break-even analysis			
Cash flow		Cost-benefit analysis			

157

Expenditure technique	Training options

158

16

How Others See Me

Purpose
- To compare the perceptions managers themselves have of how they are working with their teams to the perceptions of their team members.
- To pinpoint areas of leadership and teamwork, in light of this comparative analysis, that should be developed.

Description
This instrument is a survey that uses a rating scale to measure perceptions of management performance.

Materials
1. Sufficient copies of documents 16.1, 16.2 and 16.3.
2. A meeting room.
3. Documents 16.4a–d for analysis.

Collecting information

Methods	Benefits	Potential problems
Manager and all team members complete survey with follow-up interviews.	— All views of team members will be taken into account.	— Readiness of managers to accept feedback. — Readiness of team members to give feedback.
Managers and representative sample group of team members complete survey, with follow-up interviews.	— Less time needed for analysis of information	— Views might be unrepresentative. — Readiness of manager to accept feedback.

Methods

Manager and all team members complete survey, with follow-up interviews

1. Brief the managers and their team members on the purpose and method of the instrument and gain commitment to the approach.
2. Brief the target group of managers on accepting feedback, stressing the important steps: Be prepared to listen; be prepared to evaluate and not judge the feedback; be prepared to look for the positive and not make recriminations.
3. Distribute a copy of document 16.1 to each manager. Check for understanding and agree on a deadline for completion.
4. Encourage the team members to respond as honestly as they can, stressing that confidentiality will be maintained.
5. Distribute a copy of document 16.2 to each person and agree on a deadline for completion.
6. Collect the surveys from the team members and work out an average rating against each statement from the total responses.
7. Arrange a meeting with each manager, allowing at least one hour per meeting.
8. Ask the manager to record in column B of their survey the average rating for each statement as generated by their team members.
9. Use document 16.3 to explain the areas of teamwork and leadership referred to in the survey and give the document to the manager for future reference. Compare the manager's view of him or herself with the perceptions of team members, paying particular attention to: areas of agreement where all involved feel that improvement is required; areas where there are differences of opinion; and reasons for these differences. Encourage the manager to identify actions that will positively influence the situation. Notes can be made in column C of document 16.1.
10. Take a copy of the completed document 16.1 to analyze trends and develop a consolidated action plan. Report back to the target group of managers and their team members.

Manager and sampling of team members complete survey with follow-up interviews

Follow all the steps above, substituting a sampling of team members for the whole team. Select the sample according to the size of the team, the levels of authority, and the responsibilities represented in the roles within the team.

Analyzing results

Analysis type: NUMERICAL

Action

By following the methods above, you will complete an individual analysis of each manager. To identify trends across departments and/or the organization, compare the relationship between:

- the number of managers rating themselves higher than the average of their team and in what aspects
- the number of managers rating themselves lower than the average of their team and in what aspects
- the possible consequences of these findings on the people involved, the departments, the organization, the suppliers, the customers, and so on.

You will now be able to identify actions, including training, that will support the individual plans of each manager.

Use document 16.4a–d for this purpose. Each page analyzes one aspect of the instrument at a time: leader, doer, ideas, and builder.

Manager's copy

Consider the way you work with your team by reading the statements and rating how you match them. Using a scale of 0–5 with 5 as the highest, enter your rating in column A. You will be able to complete columns B and C at a summary meeting.

Statements	A How I see myself	B How my team sees me	C Actions
1. I go out of my way to encourage people in the group.			
2. I become impatient with people who beat around the bush.			
3. I urge the group to stick to plans and meet deadlines.			
4. When there are different opinions within the group, I encourage people to talk out their differences and reach an acceptable agreement.			
5. I can be counted on to suggest original ideas.			
6. I use humor to ease tensions and maintain good relationships.			
7. I look for common understanding before making decisions.			
8. I listen carefully to what others have to say.			
9. I avoid becoming involved in conflicts.			
10. I can quickly see what is wrong with unsound ideas put forward by others.			
11. I keep everyone informed about the whys and wherefores of a situation.			
12. I am always ready to support a suggestion for the common good.			
13. I tend to suggest plenty of ideas.			
14. I draw people out if I sense they have something to contribute.			
15. When there are problems, I push ahead and finish the job.			
16. I develop other people's ideas and improve them.			
17. I change my mind after listening to other people's points of view.			
18. I tend to seek approval and support from others.			
19. I don't mind being unpopular if it gets the job done.			
20. I go out of my way to seek ideas and opinions from other people.			
21. I am a friendly person and mix well with others.			
22. I am careful not to jump to conclusions.			
23. I am good at noticing when someone in the group is feeling resentful.			
24. I enjoy analyzing situations and weighing alternatives.			
25. I can work well with a very wide range of people.			

162

Statements	A How I see myself	B How my team sees me	C Actions
26. I have a no-nonsense style.			
27. I like to help people work well.			
28. I tend to be forceful and energetic.			
29. I like to anticipate problems and prepare for them.			
30. I press for action to make sure people don't waste time or go around in circles.			
31. I can usually persuade people to agree on a course of action.			
32. When people have second thoughts, I urge them to press on with the task in hand.			
33. I like to ponder alternatives before making up my mind.			
34. I tend to be open about how I'm feeling.			
35. People sometimes think I'm being too analytical and cautious.			
36. In discussions, I like to come straight to the point.			
37. While I'm interested in all views, I don't hesitate to make up my mind when a decision has to be made.			
38. Flippant people irritate me.			
39. I am able to influence people without harassing them.			
40. I like to think through ideas before acting upon them.			

Team member's copy

Think about how your managers work with you and the rest of the team. Read the statements and enter your rating in the box provided, using a scale of 0–5, with 5 as the highest.

	Statements	Rating
1.	They go out of their way to encourage people in the group.	
2.	They become impatient with people who beat around the bush.	
3.	They urge the group to stick to plans and meet deadlines.	
4.	When there are different opinions within the group, they encourage people to talk out their differences and come to an acceptable agreement.	
5.	They can be counted on to suggest original ideas.	
6.	They use humor to ease tensions and maintain good relationships.	
7.	They look for common understanding before making decisions.	
8.	They listen carefully to what others have to say.	
9.	They avoid becoming involved in conflicts.	
10.	They can quickly see what is wrong with unsound ideas put forward by others.	
11.	They keep everyone informed about the whys and wherefores of a situation.	
12.	They are always ready to support a suggestion for the common good.	
13.	They tend to suggest plenty of ideas.	
14.	They draw people out if they sense that they have something to contribute.	
15.	When there are problems, they push ahead and get the job done.	
16.	They develop other people's ideas and improve them.	
17.	They change their minds after listening to other people's points of view.	
18.	They tend to seek approval and support from others.	
19.	They don't mind being unpopular if it gets the job done.	
20.	They go out of their way to seek ideas and opinions from other people.	
21.	They are friendly and mix well with others.	
22.	They are careful not to jump to conclusions.	
23.	They are good at noticing when someone in the group is feeling resentful.	
24.	They enjoy analyzing situations and weighing alternatives.	
25.	They can work well with a very wide range of people.	
26.	They have a no-nonsense style.	
27.	They like to help people work well.	
28.	They tend to be forceful and energetic.	

164

	Statements	Rating
29.	They like to anticipate problems and prepare for them.	
30.	They press for action to make sure people don't waste time or go around in circles.	
31.	They can usually persuade people to agree on a course of action.	
32.	When people have second thoughts, they urge them to press on with the task.	
33.	They like to ponder alternatives before making up their minds.	
34.	They tend to be open about how they're feeling.	
35.	People sometimes think they're being too analytical and cautious.	
36.	In discussions, they like to come straight to the point.	
37.	While they're interested in all views, they don't hesitate to make up their minds when a decision has to be made.	
38.	Flippant people irritate them.	
39.	They are able to influence people without harassing them.	
40.	They like to think through ideas before acting upon them.	

Summary

The statements can be arranged under four headings:

How you see yourself as a leader.
How you see yourself as someone who finishes the job.
How you see yourself as someone who can analyze and generate ideas.
How you see yourself as a team builder.

Transfer your ratings onto the key below and add the combined ratings of the members of your team for comparison.

KEY

Item	Me	Team
1		
4		
7		
8		
11		
14		
20		
31		
37		
39		
Total		
LEADER		

Item	Me	Team
2		
3		
15		
19		
26		
28		
30		
32		
36		
38		
Total		
DOER		

Item	Me	Team
5		
10		
13		
16		
22		
24		
29		
33		
35		
40		
Total		
IDEAS		

Item	Me	Team
6		
9		
12		
17		
18		
21		
23		
25		
27		
34		
Total		
BUILDER		

Actions I will take as a result of this analysis:

Reproduced from *Training Needs Analysis—Second Edition,*
Sharon Bartram and Brenda Gibson, HRD Press.

Item	Leader		Possible consequence
	No. of managers rating self higher	No. of managers rating self lower	
1.			
4.			
7.			
8.			
11.			
14.			
20.			
31.			
37.			
39.			

Summary of findings:

167

Reproduced from *Training Needs Analysis—Second Edition*,
Sharon Bartram and Brenda Gibson, HRD Press.

	Doer		Possible consequence
Item	No. of managers rating self higher	No. of managers rating self lower	
2.			
3.			
15.			
19.			
26.			
28.			
30.			
32.			
36.			
38.			

Summary of findings:

Ideas			Possible consequence
Item	No. of managers rating self higher	No. of managers rating self lower	
5.			
10.			
13.			
16.			
22.			
24.			
29.			
33.			
35.			
40.			

Summary of findings:

	Builder		Possible consequence
Item	No. of managers rating self higher	No. of managers rating self lower	
6.			
9.			
12.			
17.			
18.			
21.			
23.			
25.			
27.			
34.			

Summary of findings:

17

How Do I See My Managers?

Purpose
To develop departmental management-development plans.

Description
The series of statements in this instrument will help senior managers identify the characteristics collectively displayed by their own managers. The process highlights both team and individual development needs.

Materials
1. Sufficient copies of documents 17.1 and 17.2.
2. A meeting room.
3. Document 17.3a and b for analysis.

Collecting information

Methods	Benefits	Potential problems
Senior manager completes the survey individually, followed by individual meeting.	— Speeds up the information-gathering process.	— Willingness to complete the survey on their own. — Unable to clarify understanding.
Survey is the basis for discussion in individual meetings.	— Able to clarify understanding.	— Time-consuming.

Methods

Senior manager completes the survey individually, followed by individual meeting

1. Brief the target group on the purpose of the instrument.
2. Give each person a copy of document 17.1 and agree on a time schedule for completion.
3. Arrange a follow-up meeting with each person, allowing up to one hour per meeting.
4. Discuss the responses and agree on a development plan.
5. Prepare a development plan (using document 17.2) for use by the senior manager in communicating with and winning commitment from the team of managers.

Survey as the basis for discussion in individual meetings

1. Brief the target group on the purpose of the instrument.
2. Arrange a meeting with each person, allowing at least two hours per meeting.
3. In each meeting, give the senior manager document 17.1 and ask him or her to comment on each characteristic in terms of evidence that this applies to their managers. Also ask them which individuals could benefit from improving their performance.
4. Encourage the senior manager to take notes.
5. Close the meeting by agreeing on a development plan for the senior manager's management team.
6. Prepare the development plan using document 17.2 for use by the senior manager communicating with and winning commitment from their team of managers.

Analyzing results

Analysis type: NUMERICAL

Action

By following the methods described above, you will complete the analysis of the information by department (which is summarized in document 17.2).

To identify trends across departments, carry out frequency counts to determine:

- the team development issues that appear most often
- the individual issues that appear most often.

Display the issues in priority order, according to the number of times they have appeared, using documents 17.3a and b for this purpose. Use a tally system to speed up the frequency count.

How do I see my managers?

Document 17.1

Think about the managers in your department. Firstly, for each of the characteristics below, place a check (✓) next to those that are in evidence. Secondly, can you think of someone who might be even more effective if they possessed those characteristics? Write their name(s) in the appropriate boxes.

Characteristics	Evident?	Name(s)
Clarifying objectives		
1. Puts specific problems into context, rather than going into irrelevant detail.		
2. Sees their own department in terms of the organization as a whole.		
3. Sets realistic and achievable objectives that meet organizational goals.		
4. Compares actual results with the objectives set in order to make improvements in the future.		
Planning		
1. Gathers information to formulate alternatives for action.		
2. Generates useful ideas and suggestions.		
3. Makes reasoned decisions.		
4. Develops both short- and long-term plans.		
Communication		
1. Listens effectively.		
2. Communicates ideas and thoughts verbally.		
3. Communicates ideas and thoughts in writing.		
4. Selects appropriate methods for communicating to all those who need to know.		
Teamwork		
1. Motivates their team and individuals.		
2. Involves others in solving problems.		
3. Influences others to gain commitment.		
4. Treats team members according to their individual needs.		
Monitoring		
1. Sets appropriate standards of work.		
2. Assesses performance against the standards.		
3. Gives both positive and critical feedback.		
4. Takes corrective action at the appropriate time.		

Characteristics	Evident?	Name(s)
<u>Training</u> 1. Identifies the training needs of staff.		
2. Plans training to meet these needs.		
3. Provides opportunities for staff to learn.		
4. Assesses the effectiveness of training.		
<u>Change</u> 1. Sees where change is necessary.		
2. Recommends changes that improve effectiveness.		
3. Responds positively to ideas for change.		
4. Creates a climate for change within their team.		

Team development issue(s)	Plan of action	Time frames

Manager's name	Development issue(s)	Plan of action	Time frames

Team issues	Tally

Priority order	Action
1.	
2.	
3.	
4.	
5.	
6.	
and so on.	

176

Individual issues	Tally

Priority order	Action
1.	
2.	
3.	
4.	
5.	
6.	
and so on.	

IV
Job Skills

This section examines all aspects of a person's job, with particular reference to knowledge and practical and behavioral skill requirements. It shows where standards are being achieved and where there are shortfalls. There are five instruments:

18. Analyzing Jobs
19. Training Needs Survey
20. Task Competencies
21. Working with Others
22. Skills Audit

The target group usually includes all employees, with the exception of senior managers for whom the instruments may not be appropriate.

Analyzing Jobs is a useful starting point: It helps managers and their staffs define the content of jobs, which can be the basis for other analyses.

Training Needs Survey involves people taking responsibility for identifying and justifying their own training needs.

Task Competencies provides the basis for departmental training records and plans, highlighting levels of skill and a person's flexibility in undertaking a number of tasks.

Working with Others explores training needs in the important area of verbal communication.

Skills Audit will help you to find out about the knowledge and skills that might presently be underutilized in your organization.

Nearly every trainer is responsible for assessing and developing employee job skills. However, before using these instruments, ask yourself if it is your responsibility. If it is, make sure that you have made the necessary preparations outlined in this training needs analysis. Using this checklist as your guide, ask yourself:

Preparation	Y	N	Action
Have you . . . . . . identified and won the support of the appropriate sponsor?			
. . . clarified your objectives? Do you know what you want to achieve by using the instrument?			
. . . assessed the potential problems of using the instruments in this target group and made contingencies for them?			
. . . considered the expectations that participation will raise, and discussed them with your sponsor and other managers?			
. . . clarified your role? Are you: —facilitating the process? —carrying out the analysis yourself?			
. . . selected the best method of collecting the information from the options given in the instrument?			
. . . prepared your briefing for the target group?			

18
Analyzing Jobs

Purpose
- To clarify the purpose of jobs.
- To analyze the knowledge and practical and behavioral skills required by job holders to perform their jobs.
- To provide a standard to compare performance against.

Description
This instrument provides a consistent method for analyzing jobs. When completed, it becomes the basis of further analysis and can be used with the remainder of the instruments in this section.

Materials
1. Sufficient copies of document 18.1.
2. Document 18.2a–c for analysis.

Collecting information

Methods	Benefits	Potential problems
Manager completes analysis for jobs in department.	— Easy to administer.	— Limited picture of what tasks are performed within each job.
Training manager or officer interviews experienced employees and manager to complete analysis.	— Thorough analysis. — Able to compare perceptions of job content. — Consistency throughout organization.	— Time to gather information.

Methods	Benefits	Potential problems
Manager and experienced job holders complete analysis for jobs in the department.	— Able to compare perceived job content with actual past performance. — Thorough analysis. — Ownership of analysis by department.	— Disruption to workplace routine.

Methods

Manager completes analysis for jobs in his or her department
1. Brief the target group on the purpose of the instrument.
2. Give each manager sufficient copies of document 18.1 and agree on a time schedule for completion and return.
3. Maintain an up-to-date record of the job's responsibilities as the basis of future training needs analysis.

Training manager/officer interviews experienced job holders and manager to complete analysis
1. Brief the target group on the purpose of the instrument.
2. Arrange meetings with experienced job holders, allowing up to one hour per meeting.
3. Discuss the responsibilities of their job and the requirements, recording their comments on document 18.1.
4. Review the completed analyses with the manager, amending where necessary.
5. Arrange for the manager to receive copies of the completed documents 18.1 so he/she can communicate with and win commitment from the job holders.
6. Maintain an up-to-date record of the job responsibilities as the basis of future training needs analysis.

Manager and experienced job holders complete analysis for jobs in the department
1. Brief the target group on the purpose of the instrument.
2. Give each manager and job holder sufficient copies of document 18.1 and make sure they agree on a time schedule to meet and complete the analysis.
3. Agree on a time schedule for the completion and return of the analysis.
4. Maintain an up-to-date record of the various job responsibilities within the department as the basis of future training needs analyses.

Analyzing results

Analysis type: NUMERICAL

Action

Further analysis of this instrument is not essential, but you may find it useful to combine it with Instrument 20 to summarize departmental tasks. You may also wish to identify areas of knowledge and practical and behavioral skills that are common to more than one job across departments in the organization in order to develop core training activities that meet training needs. Carry out frequency counts to identify those areas mentioned most often from the information generated in this instrument.

Document 18.2a–c is suggested for this purpose. Use a tally system to speed up the frequency count.

Job title ....

Task description ....

....

Knowledge requirements (what the job holder must know and understand):	1. ....
	2. ....
	3. ....
	4. ....
	5. ....
	6. ....
Practical skills—requirements (what the job holder must be able to do and demonstrate):	1. ....
	2. ....
	3. ....
	4. ....
	5. ....
	6. ....
Behavioral skills—requirements (how the job holders must conduct themselves with other people)	1. ....
	2. ....
	3. ....
	4. ....
	5. ....
	6. ....

184

Knowledge aspects common across jobs

Document 18.2a

Knowledge	Tally of times mentioned in interviews or cited

Knowledge common to more than one job

185

Reproduced from *Training Needs Analysis—Second Edition,*
Sharon Bartram and Brenda Gibson, HRD Press.

Practical skills	Tally of times mentioned or cited

Practical skills common to more than one job

Behavioral skills	Tally of times mentioned or cited

Behavioral skills common to more than one job

187

19
Training Needs Survey

Purpose
- To generate information from job holders about their perceived training needs in relation to job performance.
- To develop departmental job training plans.
- To identify common training themes across departments.
- To gauge attitudes about training.

Description
This instrument is a short survey asking the respondents to specify types of training they require in *technical, interpersonal,* and *informational* categories. It can be used in conjunction with Instrument 20 to help change attitudes towards training.

Materials
1. Sufficient copies of document 19.1.
2. A meeting room.
3. Document 19.2 for analysis.

Collecting information

Methods	Benefits	Potential problems
Postal survey by department.	— Easy to administer.	— Low response rate. — Need to chase down.
Short individual interviews by department.	— Needs of all individuals identified. — Able to clarify understanding. — Opportunity to influence attitudes.	— Time-consuming. — Disruption to workplace.

189

Methods	Benefits	Potential problems
Telephone survey by department.	— Speeds up information gathering. — Opportunity to confirm understanding. — Increases response rate.	— Could be interpreted as an impersonal approach. — Could be time-consuming if follow-up calls don't go according to plan.

Methods

Postal survey by department
1. Brief the target group on the purpose of the instrument.
2. Give each person a copy of document 19.1 and agree on a time schedule for completion and return.
3. Summarize the responses.
4. Give a copy of the completed summary to the department manager and agree on a plan of action.
5. Analyze each departmental summary and highlight common themes. Then present a plan of action to all department managers.

Short individual interviews by department
1. Brief the target group on the purpose of the instrument.
2. Interview each person, allowing at least 30 minutes per meeting. Discuss the questions on document 19.1 and record each person's responses.

Follow steps 3, 4, and 5 as above.

Telephone survey by department
1. Brief the target group on the purpose of the instrument, distributing a copy of document 19.1 to each person for their response. Arrange a convenient time to make your follow-up telephone call, allowing up to 20 minutes per call.
2. Have ready a copy of document 19.1 at the start of each call to record responses.
3. Ask the person for their response to each of the statements in turn and take notes.
4. State what you have recorded as you complete each section—technical training, interpersonal skills training, and information training—to check for understanding.
5. Thank them for their cooperation and explain that their information will be included in a departmental action plan.

Follow steps 3, 4, and 5 as in postal survey by department.

Analyzing results

Analysis type: COMBINATION

Action

Numerical analysis will enable you to summarize departmental responses. Carry out a frequency count of the number of times training is specified by respondents.

Content analysis will enable you to summarize the underlying themes and explain why respondents are specifying particular training.

Use document 19.2 to record both sets of analysis information.

You can extend your analysis to identify trends across departments and/or the organization by carrying out further frequency counts. You can also look for concurrent underlying themes; the layout in document 19.2 is easily adaptable for this purpose.

What training will help me become more effective in my job?
To answer this question, please specify the type of training you would find most helpful in the given categories. There is also space for you to explain how the specified training will help you.

Technical training (relevant to the tasks you perform in your job):

This training will help me in the following ways:

Interpersonal skills training (relevant to the interactions you have with people in order to perform your job):

This training will help me in the following ways:

Informational training (to keep you up-to-date with new developments and changes that will affect how you perform your job):

This training will help me in the following ways:

NAME ....   JOB TITLE ....

DATE ....   DEPARTMENT ....

Training	Times selected	Common benefits from the training
Technical training:		
Interpersonal skills training:		
Informational training:		

20
Task Competencies

Purpose
To identify gaps in the skill levels of job holders in a specific department. To highlight potential problems of task coverage across a department.

Description
This instrument uses a matrix to list all the tasks undertaken in a department, as well as a ranking system to state the current skill levels of job holders across these tasks. Training needs for individuals are then recorded on the matrix, along with any task coverage issues that have been highlighted. This instrument can be used in conjunction with Instrument 19 to develop training plans that have the commitment of managers and job holders.

Materials
Sufficient copies of document 20.1.

Collecting information

Methods	Benefits	Potential problems
Department manager completes matrix, reports training needs and proposed actions.	— Easy to administer.	— No involvement of job holders. — Less commitment from job holders to training.

Methods	Benefits	Potential problems
Training manager/officer and department manager jointly complete the matrix, identify training needs, and propose actions.	— Able to clarify ranking and decisions.	— No involvement of job holders. — Less commitment from job holders to training.
Department manager and job holder jointly complete the matrix, report training needs, and propose actions.	— Dialogue between managers and job holders. — Commitment from job holder and manager for training.	— Disruption to workplace routine.

Methods

Department manager completes matrix, reports training needs, and proposes actions
1. Brief the target group on the purpose of the instrument.
2. Give manager sufficient copies of document 20.1 and check for understanding. Explain that individual training needs will be shown by looking across the completed columns; task coverage issues will be highlighted by looking down the columns. Agree on a time schedule for completion and reporting back of training needs and proposed actions.
3. Agree on training needs and proposed actions, making recommendations as appropriate.

Training manager/officer and department manager jointly complete the matrix, identify training needs, and propose actions
1. Brief the target group on the purpose of the instrument.
2. Arrange a meeting with each manager, allowing at least one hour per meeting.
3. During the meeting, complete document 20.1, agreeing on training needs and actions.

Department manager and job holder jointly complete the matrix, report training needs, and propose actions

Follow steps 1 and 2 as in the first method.

3. Make sure that managers and job holders set specific dates and times for their meetings. Be available to facilitate these meetings if requested.
4. Agree on the training needs and proposed actions, making recommendations as appropriate.

Analyzing results

Analysis type: NUMERICAL

Action

The information gathered by this instrument can be used in a number of ways, depending on the needs of your organization. For example:

• to identify those tasks where there are too few staff members able to do the work without supervision
• to identify those individuals who need to broaden their experience within the department
• to identify those individuals who are sufficiently skilled to train others
• to identify potential recruitment needs
• to assist with succession planning.

Carry out frequency counts to identify these trends and to clarify priorities. Where training needs are identified, combine this instrument with Instrument 18 to clarify the content of the tasks. This will help you and others decide on appropriate training options.

DEPARTMENT: ....

Ranking values to indicate skill level:

0 = no experience at this task
1 = being trained in this task
2 = can do this task without supervision
3 = able to train others in this task

NAME	ALL TASKS CARRIED OUT IN THIS DEPARTMENT											ACTION
ACTION REQUIRED? YES/NO												

21
Working with Others

Purpose
To identify ways of improving interactions between people, enabling them to be more effective in their jobs.

Description
A pack of cards describing aspects of communication between people is used as a framework for structured discussions with job holders.

Materials
1. Sufficient copies of documents 21.1 and 21.3.
2. Document 21.2, glued onto a piece of cardboard and then cut up.
3. A meeting room.
4. Document 21.4 for analysis.

Collecting information

Method	Benefits	Potential problems
Individual discussions.	— Detailed analysis of needs.	— Time to complete.

Method

Individual discussions
1. Brief the target group on the purpose of the instrument.
2. Arrange a meeting with each person, allowing at least one hour per meeting.
3. During each meeting, give the person a copy of document 21.1 and ask them to first identify those people they work with and write their names on the document.

4. Explain that you want them to work through the pack of cards, made from document 21.2, and then answer the three questions on document 21.1 for each person they work with.

5. Use document 21.3 to record relevant information from this discussion. Give a copy of this completed document to the person at the end of the meeting.

6. Repeat steps 3, 4, and 5 until all the target group members have met. Use your notes on the documents 21.3 to produce a consolidated plan of action. Give feedback to the target group and appropriate managers on the findings.

Analyzing results

Analysis type: NUMERICAL

Action
To find out how many people require training, create a visual display to match individuals to the areas covered by this instrument, using document 21.4.

Look across the headings for each person's name and place a symbol—a dot (●), square (■), or check (✓)—in the appropriate columns to show that person's training needs. Count the number of people requiring similar types of training to determine the priorities for action.

Who are they?

Write the names of those people you must work with in order to perform your job.

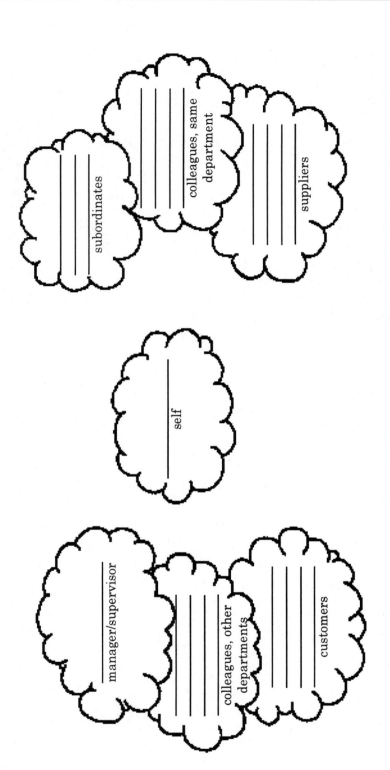

subordinates

colleagues, same department

suppliers

self

manager/supervisor

colleagues, other departments

customers

You will be given a pack of cards, each card describing an aspect of communication between people. Think about each person you work with in turn, and for each card, ask yourself these questions:

1. When do I do this?
2. How do I do this?
3. What must I do to improve?

201

Pack of cards

PERSUADING	INFLUENCING	WINNING AGREEMENT OR COMMITMENT
OBTAINING INFORMATION	GIVING INFORMATION	SAYING "NO"
DISAGREEING	MAKING SUGGESTIONS	LISTENING
QUESTIONING	STATING PROBLEMS OR DIFFICULTIES	ASKING FOR CLARIFICATION

202

Discussion summary with .... (name)

.... (department)

Person	Improvements	Action
Manager:		
Subordinates:		
Colleagues, same department:		
Colleagues, other departments:		
Customers:		
Suppliers:		

Names	Persuade	Influence	Win agree- ment	Obtain info.	Give info.	Say "no"	Disagree	Suggest ideas	Listen	Question	State problems	Ask for clarifi- cation
Total												

204

22
Skills Audit

Purpose
To generate information about the knowledge and skills individuals possess that come from previous employment or activities outside the working environment.

Description
This instrument is a short questionnaire.

Materials
1. Sufficient copies of document 22.1.
2. Document 22.2 for analysis.

Collecting information

Method	Benefits	Potential problems
Postal questionnaire.	— Easy to administer.	— Low response rate.
Telephone survey.	— Increases response rate.	— Can be time-consuming if follow-up calls do not go according to plan.
Completed individually, followed up by a meeting with department manager.	— A proactive way of using the instrument. — Opportunity to discuss points with respondent.	— Might take time.

Method

Postal questionnaire
1. Brief the target group on the purpose of the instrument.
2. Distribute a copy of document 22.1 to each person and agree on a time schedule for completion and return.
3. Maintain a record of the completed questionnaire for future reference as part of other training needs analysis activities.

Telephone survey
1. Brief the target group on the purpose of the instrument, distributing a copy of document 22.1 to each person to respond to. Arrange a convenient time to make your follow-up telephone call, allowing up to 20 minutes per call.
2. Have ready a copy of document 22.1 at the start of each call to record responses.
3. Work through the questions, asking each person for their information. Take notes.
4. Check for understanding.
5. Thank each participant for their cooperation and keep a record of the questionnaire for future reference as part of other training needs analysis activities.

Completed individually, followed up by a meeting with department manager
1. Brief the target group and their managers on the purpose of the instrument, distributing a copy of document 22.1 to each person and jointly agreeing on a deadline for them to report back to you.
2. Each respondent completes the questionnaire and then discusses it with their manager.
3. Encourage the manager to coach their staff members about the skills they possess that are not being used in their current job:

    • Does the individual want to use these skills?
    • What tasks might be delegated to the person to make more use of these skills?
    • What new tasks/activities might be developed by using the person's skills?

4. Receive a report from the manager on agreed-upon actions and keep a record of the completed questionnaires for reference.

Analyzing results

Analysis type: NUMERICAL

Action

Where further analysis is required, identify trends by matching people to the skills that are not being used. Then summarize individually-completed audits on a departmental and/or organizational basis, using document 22.2. Place a symbol—a dot (●), square (■), or check (✓)—in the appropriate columns to show which people have particular skills that are not being used.

Name ....   Job title ....

Department ....   Date ....

So that we can better develop and apply your talents in our organization, we would like to know more about you.

1.   What academic qualifications do you possess?

2.   What professional qualifications do you possess?

3.   Are you currently participating in an educational program? If so, what are you studying?

4.   Have you received any special awards? What are they?

Life experience
Do you possess skills that are not being used in your current job? You may have developed these skills at home, or from your previous employment, volunteer work, or social or community activities.

Please describe your skills under these four headings:

Working with information	Working with materials
Working with ideas	Working with people

Please continue on another sheet of paper, if necessary.

208

Name	Skills not being used					
Total						